JOURNEY TO THE LAKE DISTRICT FROM CAMBRIDGE
1779

William Wilberforce aged 21-22
Signed 'J.W. pinx'
initials of Joseph Wright of Derby

JOURNEY TO THE LAKE DISTRICT FROM CAMBRIDGE 1779

A diary written by

WILLIAM WILBERFORCE

Undergraduate of St. John's College, Cambridge

Edited by his great-great-grandson
C. E. WRANGHAM

with a foreword by
The Earl of Birkenhead

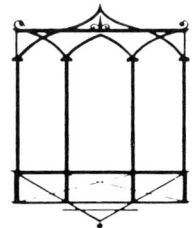

ORIEL PRESS
STOCKSFIELD
BOSTON HENLEY-ON-THAMES LONDON

TO MY COUSIN RICHARD

The Right Honourable Lord Wilberforce PC, CMG, OBE
Great-grandson of Samuel Wilberforce

*May we ever be able, my dear brother,
to keep up this unity of heart,
and may we leave something of the same
even to our children.*

Robert Wilberforce to Samuel Wilberforce.
(sons of William Wilberforce) March 1842.

IN MEMORY &
ACKNOWLEDGEMENT

THIS BOOK IS PUBLISHED
FOR THE ANNIVERSARY OF THE DEATH OF
WILLIAM WILBERFORCE
AND IN COMMEMORATION OF THE
ABOLITION OF SLAVERY IN THE
BRITISH DOMINIONS
BOTH OF WHICH TOOK PLACE 150 YEARS AGO
AND IN GRATEFUL RECOGNITION OF
THE DEVOTION
TO HIS FAMILY AND FOREBEARS OF
CUTHBERT EDWARD WRANGHAM CBE
GREAT-GRANDSON OF ROBERT WILBERFORCE
WHO DIED 10TH FEBRUARY 1982.
I WOULD LIKE TO RECORD MY GRATITUDE
TO ALL HIS FRIENDS WHO HAVE HELPED
AND ENCOURAGED ME
TO COMPLETE THIS WORK.

JEAN WRANGHAM

William Wilberforce in his twelfth year
1770

Portrait after J. Russell

CONTENTS

ILLUSTRATIONS

9

Thanks are due to the Dean and Chapter of Durham for
lending Francis Grose's *Antiquities* and Thomas West's *A
Guide to the Lakes* 1784, also to the University Library,
Durham for lending Joseph Farington's *Lakeland Views*.

FOREWORD

THIS JOURNAL, written by William Wilberforce in 1779, provides both the earliest and the fullest description of his many visits to the Lake District. It is also unusual in that on this occasion he had no preoccupations, no army of retainers and relations accompanying him, nor any plan except to immerse himself in the beauty of the scenery. He had a deep love of nature and throughout his life he could be distracted from the most urgent tasks by its beauties. He shared the preference of his contemporaries for spectacular scenery. The waterfalls, rocks, valleys, lakes and mountains of the Lake District made the rest of the English countryside seem insipid, 'peaceful' and 'rural' in contrast to the 'majestic', 'beautiful' and 'sublime' lakes. The bleaker parts of the landscape were forbidding and yet impressive; 'awful' and 'horrid' were adjectives he used to describe them. He was firm in his loyalty to the Lake District and remained faithful to it even after a visit to the greater mountains of the Swiss Alps and 'The Paradise of Interlaken'.

Another interesting characteristic of this journal is that in it Wilberforce pursues a secular approach towards beauty which would have been impossible later on. Most of his life was dominated by a deep religious faith. He underwent two conversions; the first took place when as a boy he stayed with a Methodist uncle in Wimbledon. He later remembered the general attitude towards Methodists as being comparable to that shown to Jews in *Ivanhoe*. On learning the news his mother descended, as swift and implacable as any Knight of the Temple, removed Wilberforce and set about the undermining of his faith. It was a long and agonising process which took almost three years to achieve its object. Eleven years later, in 1785, he experienced a second and permanent

11

conversion. It was the sense of purpose and duty engendered by his new faith which led him to those great causes with which we now associate his name, the campaigns against the Slave Trade and later the institution of Slavery itself. Equally it was the discipline provided by religion that enabled him to see them through.

As a convert Wilberforce looked back on the years separating his two stages of religious experience with shame, finding himself as having been at the best an idle dilettante and on occasions a dissipated wastrel. As for his way of life, 'Indolence and intemperance are its capital features'.

It is obvious and understandable that Wilberforce the convert should have exaggerated the wickedness of his unregenerate days. I also suspect that he overestimated his own idleness. The essays he wrote at Pocklington School show a precocity all the more astonishing in one who was so often to complain of the tuition there. This journal does not, in my opinion, show the same precocity, but it does reflect an enquiring mind and a tenaciousness very different from Wilberforce's own self portraits. Several of his days in the Lake District ended with him 'wet to the skin'. He must also have been cold, famished and exhausted. In these conditions it is no easy matter to settle down under the miserable light of a candle and record the events of the day at some length. To make matters worse, even in 1779 his eyesight must have been poor.

In spite of these handicaps his approach to the journal is meticulous. The reader is given detailed instructions as to his route and is even told where to stand for the best view. The dimensions of mountains and waterfalls are given or guessed at in the absence of reliable information; old country tales are retold. It reads as if he was preparing a guide book to the Lakes or doing an exercise as a young pupil of Repton's.

This might be what one would expect from an undergraduate's diary of a visit to the Lakes. But for Wilberforce to write like this was only possible in the brief period when he had no deep religious convictions. After 1785 and his second conversion any journal of his, whatever the subject, would have contained a mass of religious reflections. Religion, in his view, must be allowed to pervade every part of life. Mountains, views and waterfalls would be described not only as sublime and majestic, but also as evidence of God's goodness, as reminders (as he later wrote of another form of natural beauty) 'of the dispensations of Divine Providence first breaking on the glorified eye, when they shall fully unfold to the view, and appear as beautiful as they are complete'. The difference in approach is a vivid illustration of the change in Wilberforce. It is fascinating to have this journal to compare with his later writings. It also sheds some light on a period of his life about which too little is known.

November 1979   *Robin Birkenhead*

Lord Birkenhead (Robin Furneaux) is the author of *William Wilberforce*, 1974.

William Wilberforce in 1789
Portrait by John Rising

INTRODUCTION

'My Father's account of his first visit to the Lakes when at College.' This had been written by Robert Wilberforce on the outside of a scruffy roll of papers. It turned out to consist of 34 sheets, some torn, some tattered, closely written in ink with few alterations or additions, but often hard to read. Entries seem to have been made consecutively save for Friday 10th September, which occupied a single sheet obviously written a little later. Help in deciphering the words has been rendered by Mrs. Alison Borer, to whom every reader, like myself, owes much. Her help was always laborious and often brilliant. Conversion from transcript to typescript has been the patient and invaluable work of Mrs. Linda Baldry.

Nowhere in this account is the year specified, but such days as are dated prove it conclusively to have been 1779. Wilberforce himself mentions visiting the Lakes two years earlier, i.e. 1777, in which year also he would have been 'at College'. Furthermore, writing from Muncaster Castle, Ravenglass, on 1st October 1818 to his cousin, Samuel Smith MP, he recalls their joint visit to that neighbourhood 'two and forty years ago', in particular Wastdale Head, 'the valley in which we slept, or rather pass'd the night, in the same Wooden Crib, after piercing thro' the Gorge of Borodale'. If correctly dated, that visit took place in 1776, and the current visit would therefore be his third. Robert and his brother, Samuel, in their biography merely state that a visit to a College friend had made their father well acquainted with Westmorland.

This then is William Wilberforce's last Long Vacation from Cambridge. There on a July morning he has mounted his horse to start north on a leisurely journey for a holiday with friends in the Lakes. Is it perhaps a final fling? Twelve

15

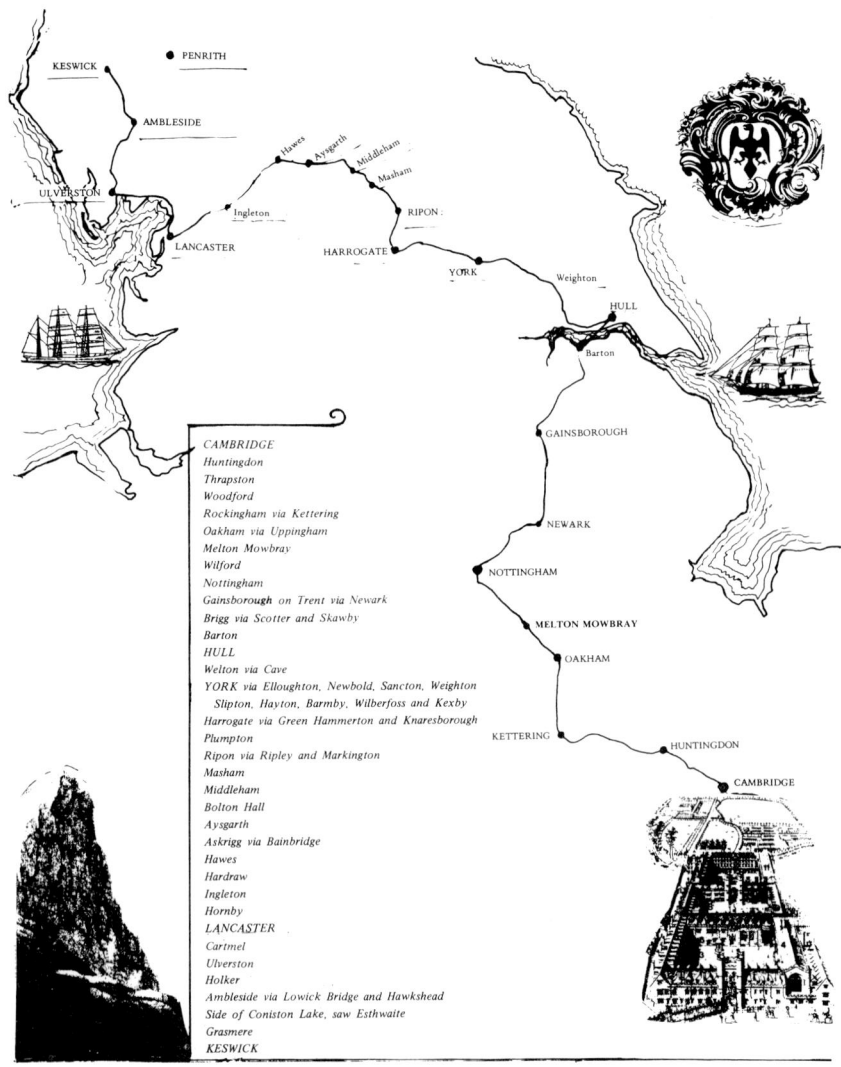

KESWICK

PENRITH

AMBLESIDE

Hawes Aysgarth Middleham
Masham

ULVERSTON

Ingleton

RIPON

LANCASTER

HARROGATE

YORK Weighton

HULL

Barton

GAINSBOROUGH

CAMBRIDGE
Huntingdon
Thrapston
Woodford
Rockingham via Kettering
Oakham via Uppingham
Melton Mowbray
Wilford
Nottingham
Gainsborough on Trent via Newark
Brigg via Scotter and Skawby
Barton
HULL
Welton via Cave
YORK via Elloughton, Newbold, Sancton, Weighton
    Slipton, Hayton, Barmby, Wilberfoss and Kexby
Harrogate via Green Hammerton and Knaresborough
Plumpton
Ripon via Ripley and Markington
Masham
Middleham
Bolton Hall
Aysgarth
Askrigg via Bainbridge
Hawes
Hardraw
Ingleton
Hornby
LANCASTER
Cartmel
Ulverston
Holker
Ambleside via Lowick Bridge and Hawkshead
Side of Coniston Lake, saw Esthwaite
Grasmere
KESWICK

NEWARK

NOTTINGHAM

MELTON MOWBRAY

OAKHAM

KETTERING

HUNTINGDON

CAMBRIDGE

16

months hence the shades of the prison-house would have been taking shape. He would have gone down from Cambridge, bent upon entering politics. Already he would have been canvassing the electorate in his native town of Hull, before going on to canvass the Hull voters in London, where he would spend long July evenings in the stuffy gallery of the old House of Commons, listening to the vituperations of Burke and Fox against Lord North in the Debates on the American War. Here he would find company in a Cambridge acquaintance, William Pitt, so soon to become a life-long friend. Within a matter of months they would both be elected MP. Within 5 years Pitt would be writing as Prime Minster to congratulate Wilberforce (each of them then 24 years old) on his tour de force in securing nomination as one of the two MPs for Yorkshire, 'Knights of the Shire'. The next year (1785) would see Wilberforce on his spiritual road to Damascus, which fundamentally changed his life for ever. During the following two years (1786, 1787) his commitment to Parliamentary leadership of an Anti-Slave Trade campaign would be made and publicized.

All this within eight years! But now, 35 miles on from Cambridge, the rider is reaching Woodford, near Thrapston in Northamptonshire, to stay four nights — apparently at the Plough Inn. Perhaps he has friends in the vicinity. Thence a late afternoon ride takes him 18 miles on to the inn at Rockingham for the night, and next day he covers some 41 miles through Oakham and Melton Mowbray to Wilford, just south of Nottingham. Seemingly he stays a spell at Wilford (still a district of the greatest charm some sixty years ago), but his movements at this stage are conjectural, for 11 days pass unrecorded before he leaves Nottingham. Possibly he has been spending some time with a College friend, Gerard Edwards, whose family had property in the neighbourhood. From Nottingham the boat takes him 70-80 miles down the Trent — presumably with a night on board — for a smelly night at Gainsborough and thence after a journey of 35 miles on horseback he arrives via the Barton ferry at Hull.

There he spends 16 nights, No. 25 High Street being the family home at which his mother and sister were living. The following 2 days at Welton, 10 miles up the Humber, are occupied perhaps in inspecting family property. From Welton to York, 31 miles, and on to Harrogate, 21 miles, no stop is mentioned. The period from leaving Welton to departing from Harrogate is shown as 9 days, much if not all of which may have been spent perhaps at Harrogate, as a base for local explorations: there is no mention of visiting family friends or his near-by family estate at Markington (he was not much interested in it). On his 20th birthday (August 24th) he passes through Markington, without comment, to Ripon, Masham and Middleham, 31 miles in all. Here he enters Wensleydale, and at once he becomes much taken with it, as indeed were Wordsworth and Turner, respectively, some twenty years later. Apparently he has been travelling in a chaise from Hull — perhaps having left his horse at home there. At Middleham, however, he seems likely to have acquired a local horse, whose hooves were accustomed to the stony terrain. After a night at Middleham he moves for the next night a few miles up the dale to Bolton Hall, occupied by the hospitable ('chocolate, fruit') steward of the Duke of Bolton. He saunters on, sight-seeing, a further 10 miles up the dale to find highly acceptable quarters in an Askrigg inn for the next 3 nights. Finally his stay in Wensleydale ends with a rough ride of 20 miles up and over the high Fells by the Roman track — the only route before the turnpike road — to Ingleton, there to spend a comfortless night and a frustrating day awaiting a chaise to carry him on to Hornby and Lancaster.

Now at last he comes to the Lakes. He starts off on horseback over Morecambe Sands — notoriously treacherous, but then a regular route — to Ulverston. Thence he goes up the road on the west side of Coniston to Ambleside, 43 miles on a very fine day — what a wonderful ride it must have been! Next day he soon reaches his holiday base, Keswick, 17 miles off, to meet his friends as planned. It is September 3rd and he had left Cambridge on July 10th, 410 miles in all, 75 by water, 110 by chaise and 225 on horseback. Some two-thirds of the time he had spent making visits en route, and his actual travelling averaged about 26 miles a day.

Of those he met in the Lakes only two are certainly known. Thomas Gisborne was a College friend, who became the deeply conscientious 'squarson' of Yoxall Lodge in Needwood Forest and an intimate, warm and sympathetic fellow-campaigner for Wilberforce. William Cookson was another College friend, engaged in a mercer's business in Penrith, whose sister had married John Wordsworth, and given birth to the poet at Cockermouth nine years earlier. Some of the other names quoted refer perhaps to residents, for Wilberforce had been there previously and Cookson lived not far away. There follow the accounts of their excursions, described with romantic zest.

Wilberforce's early attachment to the Lakes ripened into a deep and lasting affection. Writing in 1808 to his dear friend Lord Muncaster, who lived there, he ended, 'Farewell, my friend; I wish I were with you: my mouth waters to think of your rocks and mountains, and shady walks'. In the same year he conveyed specific directions to a friend starting on a northern tour, recommending approach to the Lakes through Wensleydale:-

> ... thence to Keswick, where you must stay two or three days, and especially take a round through Borrowdale and Buttermere, and Crummock Water, and through Newlands Vale; also you must go the whole road from Keswick to Ambleside; it is the most delightful ride in England. If you are a mountaineer, cross Hard Knot and Wrynose to Lord Muncaster's, who, from what I will immediately write to him, will receive you with his characteristic hospitality; and from Muncaster, if you really have a mind to see the interior of the country, go by Wastdale and over the Styehead into Borrowdale, and thence to Keswick again; it is the very deliciae of mountain scenery.

On October 1st 1818, the same day that he wrote from Muncaster Castle to his cousin Samuel Smith, he wrote also (in a letter most kindly furnished by Mrs. Linda Grobstein from New York) to Marianne Francis, an intimate family friend:-

> Ever since I first conversed with my Wife, and that my children were capable of understanding me, I have been speaking of the Scenery of this Region of Wonders, in terms of the highest Eulogy; yet so far from being disappointed they all declare that their Utmost Expectations have been surpassed. And I for my own part, I must say that I do not find my Admiration & Love of

19

this Earthly Paradise to have owed any part of their force to a youthful fancy — but even now, when all my faculties are bien usées, *they, not the faculties alas!, but the Admiration and Love are as great as ever.*

Later still, in his mid-sixties, he wrote to Lady Olivia Sparrow:-

It is not a mere imagination that in the case of a cold-blooded creature like myself, a country of lakes and rocks and mountains . . . appears to call forth all the affections into augmented animation . . . When I was a very young man (a very young man, understand), I was always in danger of falling in love when I was an inhabitant of romantic countries . . .

Regrettably, no signs of such romances appear. But, far from being cold-blooded, Wilberforce was characterized as having quicksilver in his veins!

The especial delight in Borrowdale, that this journal shows, has descended through his family. Robert's son, Edward, records in detail a high-light of his boyhood as the holiday on which his father and his uncle, Samuel, took him to Grasmere and Keswick. Edward's eldest son, Lionel, one of the most proficient climbers of his age, is commemorated in Rosthwaite Chapel, which Wilberforce mentions, for his love of that countryside — 'a great grand-son of William Wilberforce MP, The Emancipator, whose truly Christian spirit he inherited'. And that affection remains among his posterity today.

We take leave of Wilberforce at Ambleside on 25th September. Perhaps his stay there introduced him to Rayrigg, the manor house by Lake Windermere, of which he took a 7-year lease the following year. But now he would soon have to be heading south to begin his final terms at Cambridge, two hundred years ago.

C. E. WRANGHAM

September 1979
Rosemary House, Catterick, Yorkshire.

Rosthwaite, Borrowdale from the road
to Watendlath. On the left is the
chapel mentioned on page 20.
After Thomas Allom

NOTE. In the text of the Diary which follows the original spelling, punctuation and abbreviations have been preserved as far as possible.

July 10th

From Cambridge to Huntingdon 16 miles, the Country miserably bad, a dead Flat almost the whole way; from Huntingdon through Thrapston to Woodford 18½ miles — Thrapston is a small Market Town, in which there is carried on an inconsiderab. Woolen manufactory —

The Face of the Country, in general but indifferent except where it is diversified by some woods of the Duke of Manchester's & St Barnards some of the finest Crops of Wheat I ever saw — The Civility of the County People between Hunt'n & Thrap: struck me after my having lately a Resiven of London or Cambridge. Throughout all Northamptons: see the Woolen manufac: is carried on especially at & about Kettering, there is also dair work, in which Children can earn from to shillings a Week — July 14th From Woodford to Rockingham 18 miles — The Road goes through Kettering (which is 8 miles distant from Woodford) & on each side of it one sees remarkably fine Crops of Wheat, Oats, & Clover — The Spire of the Chu: at Kettering is wonderfully light & taper — at Kettering there are Assemblies in the Winter — after Almost the whole way from Kettering to Rockingham lies thro' the Foresters, where there are a prodigious number of Deer. The forest without but few Breaks extend through almost the whole County. Riding in it was very plea—

THE DIARY 1779

July 10th

From Cambridge to Huntingdon 16 miles north. The
Country miserably bad, a dead Flat almost the whole way.
From Huntingdon through Thrapston to Woodford
(Plough) 18½ miles. Thrapston is a small Market Town, in
which there is carried on an inconsiderable woolen
manufactory. The Face of the Country in general but
indifferent except where it is diversified by some woods of
the Duke of Manchester's and Sir Robert Barnard's. Some
of the finest crops of Wheat I ever saw. The Civility of the
Country People between there & Thrapston struck me after
my having been lately a Resident of London & Cambridge.
Throughout all Northamptonshire the woolen Manufactory
is carried on especially at & about Kettering, and there is
also Lace made, in which children can earn from —
to — shillings a Week.

July 14th

From Woodford to Rockingham 18 miles. The Road goes
through Kettering (which is 8 miles distant from Woodford)
& on each side of it one sees remarkably fine crops of
Wheat & Oats & Clover. The spire of the Church at
Kettering is wonderfully light & taper'd; there are
Assemblies in the Winter. Almost the whole way from
Kettering to Rockingham lies thro' the Forest, in some
parts of which there are a prodigious number of Deer. The
Forest with but few Breaks extends through almost the
whole County. Riding in it was very pleasant but
unfortunately it was Night before I reached Rockingham, &
I missed the Sight of an exceedingly fine Prospect which my
Landlord informed me there was from the Hill which
overlooks the Village. The Village of Rockingham is a very
inconsiderable one; the Marquis takes his Title from thence
but the Seat & Park are at present Lord Sondes's.[1]

July 15th

From Rockingham to Oakham 11 miles. The Road is
through Uppingham. As soon as you enter Rutlandshire the
Country becomes very hilly & the Hills being almost
wellwooded have a beautiful appearance — no requisite for
a fine Prospect is wanting but Water. Uppingham stands
very high & the Spire of its Church is seen at a great
distance. Betwixt Uppingham & Oakham on the right is
Burleigh on the Hill. The Woods rising up the declivity
have a good Effect. In the Park are some fine Views &
large respectable Trees. Oakham is a very pretty but
diminutive Capital of a diminutive County. The Land in
Rutlandshire is generally poor. The Inhabitants furnish
about the full complement, 1 in 12, to the Militia. From
Oakham to Melton Mowbray 10 miles. The County still
better to look at than have one's Estate in, & there are
some very extensive & tolerably pretty Views. From Melton
to Wilford betwixt 19 & 20 miles. One frequently ascends
Hills from which one can see the Country for an immense
distance. There is here but little Wood — but from one of
the Hills there is a very agreeable Prospect, in which from
the side of a Hill upon whose ascent the Road goes one has
a fine view of a slope rising abruptly, covered with
underwood, & some hay-rick meadows in the Vale below.
There are some high hills visible at a great distance on the
left about $\frac{1}{2}$ way betwixt Melton & Nottingham. Melton is
an inconsiderable little Town. Mr. Menell frequently hunts
in its neighborhood in the Winter. The Road to Nottingham
is in some parts a very bad one. The latter part of it goes
thro' the Forest which, however pleasant it may formerly
have been when Robin and little John lived there under the
Greenwood Tree, is now nothing but one disagreeable wide
extended Heath without any thing to diversify the Scene or
render the prospect agreeable. Some of the Dukes' Parks are
in the Forest which are exceptions. Clifton, about 2 miles
from Wilford, is the Seat of Sir Jervas Clifton,[2] and there is
a Walk, where you go at the Bottom of a wellwooded Hill
by the Side of the Trent, which is exceedingly well worth
seeing. N.B. Walk at the Bottom not at the Top of the Hill.
Above Wilford is a Hill on which Sir Jervas has built a

Burleigh House
After Thomas Allom

The Trent at Arnold, Nottingham
A water colour by Richard Parkes Bonington
as a child, probably in 1808
when he was seven years old.

Nottingham and its environs
After Thomas Allom

Lincoln from the River Witham
After Thomas Allom

Summer House from whence there is a very extensive View; one sees Lincoln Minster etc. The prettiest objects in it are Bunny Park[3] the Seat of Sir Thos. Perkins, & Colwick[4] that of Mr. Musters. An old Church at Bunny & some rude Houses just under the Wood & the naked Hill on one side form a very picturesque Landscape. This should be seen in the Morning. Nottingham: Trade, Castle, Burgesses' Pasture Right.

July 26th & 27th

From Nottingham to Gainsbrough by the Trent, computed to be 70 or 80 miles. From Nottingham till one comes within 4 miles of Newark the Voyage answers very well, & there are a few very pretty Views particularly at Colwick, Radcliffe &c., but afterwards there is little to attract a stranger's attention. The Trent about 10 miles from Gainsbrough makes two remarkable Bends which are called Burton Round & No Man's Friend. You are at the first of them within fifty yards of a Part of the River which you do not reach till you have gone near two miles. The Country about Gainsbrough execrable, & the Inn we were at (which is said to be better than the other) miserably bad & dirty as indeed is the whole Town. I open'd the Window for a little fresh air, & the Smell which immediately filled the room was nasty beyond description. Gainsbrough: Trade, Staffordshire Lincolnshire etc.

July 28th

From Gainsbrough to Brigg 18 miles. The Country in general very bad & not a single good View. One passes over two very extensive moors. The Road goes through Scotter and comes into the Lincoln Road at Scawby. From Brigg to Barton, north, 12 miles. The Country pretty for Lincolnshire & a very rich cornfield call'd Barton field which was but lately inclos'd. From Barton over the Humber to Hull 5 miles. The Shore in general very bad, the prospect from the Road tolerable of Welton, Melton & Ferriby. The Humber is here reckon'd 3 miles directly over. Hull: Trade, Docks, Baltic, Dantzig etc.

Saturday August 13th

From Hull to Welton 10 miles north. The Villages on the Banks of the Humber about $\frac{3}{4}$ of a mile from it are in general pretty, & Mr. W's[5] improvements at Welton a great Honor to his Taste. From his Fields as well as from the Road betwixt Welton & Cave the junction of the Trent & Ouse makes a very agreeable Prospect.

Monday August 15th

From Welton to York 31 miles north through Elloughton, Newbald, Sancton, Weighton, Shipton, Hayton, Barmby, Wilberfoss[6] & Kexby. When you lose sight of the Humber the Country begins to look very indifferent, & from Weighton to York 19 miles the Ride does not afford a single Object (except a small View of the Wolds) that would reward ones looking to the right Hand or to the left. Mem. always to sleep this Stage. A little before you come to Weighton you see Londsbrough, the Duke of Devonshire's, on the right at the foot of the Wolds, & just beyond Hayton you see also on your right Hand Sir Willm. Anderson's Woods at Kilwick & the town of Pocklington,[7] which the Road leads to which turns off at the new Inn. From York to Harrogate 21 miles north, through Green Hamerton & Knaresbrough. Harrogate is situate upon the Edge of a very extensive Moor & you cannot ride or walk out but upon a hard, stony Road. Nothing can be more desolate than the natural situation of it though there are some pretty places in the Neighborhood. Knaresbrough is a very neat well built Town. But there are several delightful Walks by the River Side all of which a stranger should see as well as the Castle, & Castle Yard. The dropping Well is very pretty but nothing uncommon. A stranger must go above it to one of the Walks by the river. From Harrogate see Plumpton,[8] Mr. Jan. Lascelles's. The Green Dragon the best House. Excursion into Craven or Wensley dale would well reward the Traveller. Harrogate is 11 miles from Rippon, & 16 from Leeds.

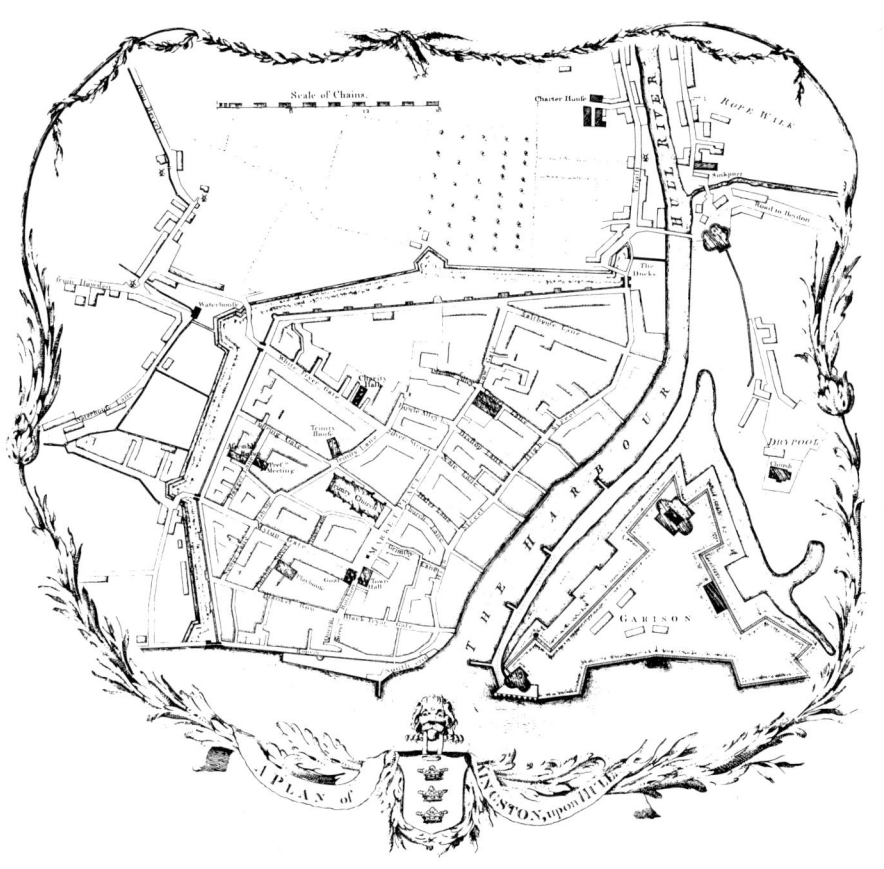

Hull, home of the Wilberforce Family
From *A Survey of the County of Yorkshire* by Thomas Jefferys 1775.

August 24th

From Harrogate to Rippon through Ripley & Markington.
Sir John Ingleby's at Ripley. Beautiful Walk by the River
— mem. to ride down the Bed of it when I next go that
Way. Went from Rippon to Masham 10 miles north.
Stopped to see the last great View at Hackfall, which any
Passer-by may see in ten minutes, who has not time to go
thro' the whole. The ride from Rippon to Masham through
the finest Country I ever saw in England, hilly, well
wooded, water'd & very fertile land, but not a Corn
Country. Masham an exceedingly well built pretty little
Town. Mr. Danby who lives at Swinton within a mile of it
has £5000 a year all about him, which he lets in small
Farms from year to year. From Masham to Middleham 10
miles, north. Got out of my Chaise about half way to see
the Ruins of Jervaux Abbey, as it is worth every Traveller's
while to do. It was dark before I left it & the Moon shone
very bright. There are no Arches remaining entire but a
great part of the Walls. It is rather difficult to get to it. It
was formerly a very extensive one. Mem. to look for it in
Grose's *Antiquities* & Tanner's *Notitia Monastica*. There are a
great number of Coal Mines near Masham chiefly
belonging to Mr. Danby, one of whose workmen in the Coal
Mines has a great genius for Husbandry: he has taken from
the Barren Moor (which comes very near Masham &
almost joins upon the Road all the Way to Middleham) 40
or 50 acres, which he has cultivat'd, inclos'd, hoed, burnt
etc. with his own Hands without any Help & brought to a
high State of Improvement. The Country People tell you
that one might go from Masham into Scotland without
going off the Moors. Middleham is a small Town
remarkable for nothing so much as its Castle which though
in Ruins retains the Marks of having been a very grand &
strong one. It is said that is was destroyed in Oliver
Cromwell's time.

August 25th

Saw Middleham Castle, climb'd with some difficulty to the
Top of one of its old Towers & had a delightful View of the

Middleham Castle
From Francis Grose's *Antiquities*

Jervaulx Abbey
From Francis Grose's *Antiquities*

Country thro' which I had come. The Castle has been a very large one. (Lord Bruce Aylesbury has a very large Estate £7000 a year near Masham, Hackfall, Middleham; Jervaux Abbey belongs to him, more of which would have been standing, if the farmers had not pull'd some of it down to build their Houses with the Stone. Lord Aylesbury has now forbid that Practice, but has not been in that Country for 10 or 13 years. In all this Country Cattle Horses & Sheep are bred in great numbers, & it is almost all grassland.) Stand on the West Side of the Castle about 100 yards from it behind a small Bush & there is a remarkable Eccho which will repeat some sounds as far as six very distinctly after you. Provisions are cheap all thro' this Country & the air about Middleham particularly healthful. There are many old People in it. Land lets very high. In the Castle Yard I met two old men, one upwards of 80 was very stout, the other 76 was a Barber & shaved as well as ever. In Middleham are about 200 families, & it is a deanery. It is a very good Place to fix one's Quarters at, when one goes to shoot Moor Game.[9] Went from Middleham up Wensley dale 3 miles north to see Bolton Hall, a seat of the Duke of Bolton's where his Steward Mr. Maude resides. The opening of Wensley dale is beyond measure beautiful. High Hills and sometimes rocky crags inclose a Valley where the fields after a month's drought have more Verdure than I ever saw in any other in the opening of Spring. At the Bottom of this Valley (a pretty wide one) winds the Eure, which takes its Rise in Cotter beyond Hawes & joins the Ouse below Boroughbridge; & on each side of it are numbers of Villages, the white Spires of whose Churches, peeping at Intervals from the Wood, have a most pleasing Effect. This Vale takes its name from a small Village at the opening of it. Almost immediately upon your entering it Pen Hill is on your Right & continues so for many miles. Thro' Wensley to Bolton Hall 5 miles. Mr. Maude met me on the steps & shewed me the House & Garden in which are nothing worth seeing. Chocolate & fruit; ask'd me to stay to dinner & went with me himself round the Park. In it are some beautiful Views of the green fields, the River wooded on each Side, the villages of West Witton & Sunny Wit[10] under Penhill in front, and behind

The Church and Bridge at Wensley
From Francis Grose's *Antiquities*

Bolton Castle, Wensleydale
From Francis Grose's *Antiquities*

the House Leyburn with a very Gigantic rocky Hill the top of which looks like the Walls of some old Castle. An opening through the Trees gives one a sight of Bolton Castle. The Garden is quite in the old formal taste with Terraces one above another on made foundations and a fish Pond. Fruit does not appear to be good in the Vale by the Specimen I saw, though there is much wall fruit against the Walls of the Terraces. Went after dinner to see Aysgarth Force, but it was nearly dark before I got there. Return'd & slept at Bolton Hall.

Thursday 26th

Went after Breakfast to Aysgarth. Saw Bolton Castle in Ruins & the Room in which Mary was confined a poor dark Place with but one Window in it. From the top of the Castle a fine View of Wensleydale. From Bolton Hall to Aysgarth 5 miles north. Very little Water in the River so saw the Cascade at a disadvantage, but from the surrounding scenery the Scene is a delightful one. The great fall of Water is near Carperby where is a tolerable Inn. The River falls from Rock to Rock, sometimes for several yards at a time. The sides are like the white Walls of a Castle, & the Bed of the River is like a complete Rock. There are deep and sometimes large holes worn in it which are done by the Stones in a full season whirling round at the Bottom. Walk up the Bed of the River, not at the top of the Hill, till you come near Aysgarth Church. You then see through the one Arch of a beautiful Bridge a continuation of little Waterfalls. The inside top of the Arch looks covered with Petrifactions, & the View is most beautifully picturesque. On the other side of the Bridge walk till the Shore becomes flat. The River is inclosed on the South side just above the Bridge by a very high Hill completely cover'd with Wood, somewhat like Mr. Port's but not so fine, amongst which you see many large fragments of Rock which look like the Battlements of some old Castle, high bosom'd in lofty Trees. Many Trout in the River, & below the Carperby fall (they cannot get over it) great Quantities of Salmon Smelts. The 1st Duke of Bolton was created by Willm. 3d. When Marquis of Winchester in James 2d's time, he was

34

Aysgarth Bridge Falls

From *A six month tour through the North of England 1770*
by Arthur Young who made this sketch

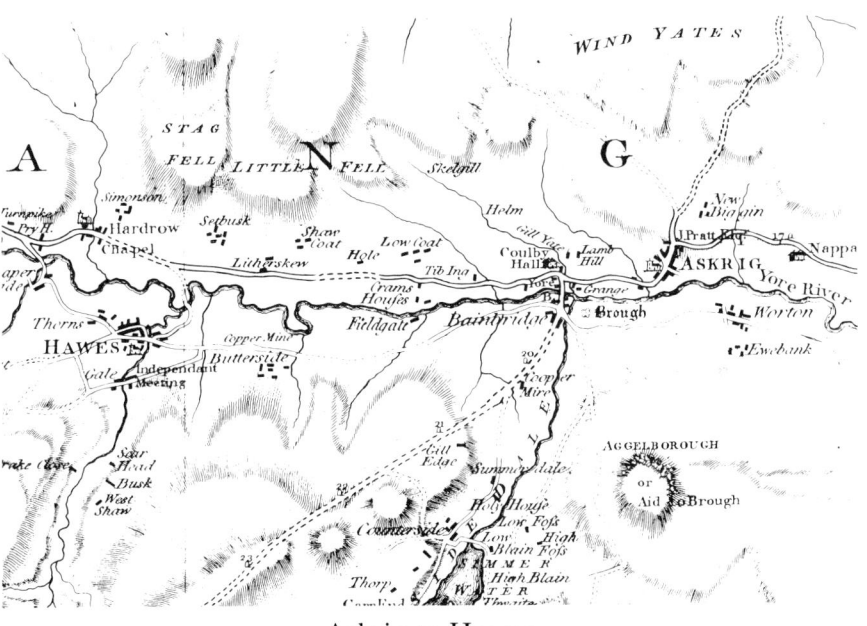

Askrig to Hawes

From *A Survey of the County of Yorkshire* 1775

suspected of holding correspondence with the Prince of Orange & that he might blind the Court he acted madness. He us'd often to hunt by Torch-light, would retire to a little Castle which he had built in the Park, the Ruins of which are still visible, and there play his fooleries. When Sir T. Knolles came to ask his assistance for James, the Marquis who had been advertised of his coming was found riding upon a stick. This farce he continued for 3 or 4 years & in his Patent[11] of Creation are these Words, that like Brutus he feign'd himself mad, & like Brutus sav'd his country. From Aysgarth to Askrigg thro' Bainbridge 6 miles & ½ north. The View of Askrigg Church pretty from the opposite side of the Water.

Friday 27th

Saw Mill Gill & Whitfell Gill. You go into a dell inclos'd by high Crags at the Bottom of which runs a clear stream. At Mill Gill the dell goes in 3 or 400 yards. The Rocks at the side jutting out like Buttresses have a fine Effect & the View of them is here & there interrupted by Trees and Shrubs, which seem to grow without any Soil. At the End is the Waterfall which falls from Rock to Rock & has a much finer effect than if it was one fall. It seems to have worn the Top a little as just the Part where the Water comes down is lower than the Rock at each side and work'd in. Whitfell Gill is one sheet of Water falling into a kind of Bason full 20 yards. You go into it above a Quarter of a Mile. To all these Waterfalls, which are exceedingly well worth seeing, go at the bottom of the dell stepping from stone to stone. You lose half their Beauty seeing them from above. Desire to be carried through some of Mr. Pratt's[12] clover to have a View of Mill Gill all at once & quite unexpectedly. Went from Askrigg to Hawes 5½ miles. The Road and the country much the same but hardly so good as before. Askrigg is a small town with a very inconsiderable market: in its neighborhood and in the Place itself the manufactory is entirely that of knit stockings, mittens etc. Old & young work at it alike & after the farmers' servants have finished their day's Work, they are often set to it by their Masters. One sees the Milk Maids knitting as they go & come back from the cow & the Country People at market employed in the same manner. Their stockings go to Leeds, Wakefield & Manchester. Trade decreased lately. The Business is not carried on in the same manner as at Nottingham: here the Common People buy wool in the neighborhood or at Newcastle, which they themselves work into Yarn; they then make the Stockings and sell them to the Wholesale Dealers, who sell them again at an advanced Price. Kirby Stephen wool market. Very little worsted used. The Yarn Stockings are made from 7d. to 10s 6d. a Pair, the Average price 5s.

Throughout Wensleydale the land is very rich, almost entirely grazing land & sells from £2 10s. to £4 an acre. A great Quantity of Butter made & of Cheese chiefly of the thin sort, which goes by the Waggon to York, Leeds & Wakefield. 2 cows are reckon'd to give in a season 3 firkins of Butter (36 lib.[13] a firkin) at the same time that their Milk $\frac{1}{2}$ new $\frac{1}{2}$ old is used in Cheeses. The firkins of a good dairy will sometimes sell for 27s. or 30s. a piece. Some Lead Mines in Wensleydale, the 2 principal ones at Welgroves or Hawbanks, & Bobscar near Redmire. If I suspect that there are Mines in any Place I go to the Owner of the soil and give him a trifle to ratify the Agreement which is made between us, which is that I work the Mine he having every 5th Pig free of all Charges. The quantity of Land is defin'd by the Words of the Agreement — so many Meers[14] of land. If the Limestone has a mixture of Lead in it, it is a sign of there being good mines beneath. They then (almost always from the top of the Hill) bore 20 or 30 or as low as 7 or 8 fathoms, & if they be incommoded by Water they drive a Level into the side of the hill to let it off. When driving or sinking, the Wages £1, £2 or £3 a fathom. When they have found vein they follow it, & believe from Observation that it is better from East to West than from North to South. When they dig the Ore, the Workmen have so much a ton according to the goodness of the Vein. They have now at Bobscar 18s. a ton, at Welgroves 6 pounds.[15] Their Wages if by day or Week about 9s. The Workmen pound it small & wash it. It is then carried in small Bags, 2 on a Horse, to the smelting mill (there is one at Preston) & made into Pigs & goes thence to Yarm, Hull, Stockton by

Land Carriage; at present it sells for £12 or £14 formerly for £17 or £18 a Ton. The Hole is in general 1½ yard high and 1 yard wide. The Master finds tools, the Men Powder for blasting & Candles. The Mine at Welgroves nearly exhausted, has been worked 400 years. The Employment is esteemed a very unwholesome one. An Asthma is the complaint it generally brings on. They seldom live till 60. Never any damps[16] in their Mine.

In the Lead Mines in Wensleydale there is said to be in the ore a great Proportion of silver, which taken out, the Lead becomes very indifferent. A Person came some years ago to one of the Smelting Mills & desired leave to put his Stick which he had previously prepar'd by some Chymical Process into the melted Ore, which being granted he having put it in drew it out again cover'd round by pure Virgin Silver. Upon consultation he was immediately offered £100 a year if he would stay & practise his Art to their advantage which he refused but would for £500 a year. They upon consideration did not think it worth while.

Hawes a far smaller Town than Askrigg. The Market is more considerable. Slept there &

August 28th

on Saturday morning went before Breakfast to see Hardrow Scar about a mile & ½ off. It is a Waterfall of the same kind as Whitfell and Mill Gills, but the fall is much greater, & the Rocks at the side higher, though not so picturesque as those at Mill Gill. The Dell is wider & at the end opens into a longer semicircle than the others. In all of them imagine yourself at the bottom of a dock[17] which has a rounded End, & you conceive their Shape. The Water falls into a Bason at once 35 yards & over the Bason the rock hangs over considerably, which looks dreadful from below, as it seems to have nothing to support it, & is not in rough Pieces but in one sheet as if hewn or made by Art. It answers very well to go as near the Water at the side as possible as it looks much higher then, than when you view it in front. In the Great Frost, 1739, the Water froze as fast as it came down till it made an immense Column of Ice 35 yards high

& 76 round. The sides also of the dell were all cover'd with Ice, which at the thaw fell down with a thundering noise, & the Part of the Rock which impends over the Bason which constantly distills water was cover'd with long small Icicles reaching from the Top to the Bottom. The Appearance is said to have been most beautiful. At a public house close to the Bridge at Hardrow get a man to shew the Scar, which is just by, & he remembers & will give an account of the Icicles. The Roads throughout this country are so hard that it is advisable to buy a Horse in it which being us'd to them will go on them with speed & safety. At Hardrow is a Methodist Meeting House, & a good many Quakers.

Went from Hawes by Simmer Water to Askrigg about 7 miles. It is a Lake about 2 miles round or hardly so much, in a Valley not near so pretty as the generality in this country, as you see little but black nasty Moors. The best View of it is on the Road to it from Askrigg, about $2\frac{1}{2}$ miles from Askrigg. There it looks pretty enough & larger than in any other situation as you see it in Length. It is worth while seeing it that way, as there is a good country on your left. In it there is said to be plenty of Trout but the Season is over by the middle of August. There are Pike in it too. All the inhabitants who live in the neighborhood are Quakers. A Brother of Dr. Fothergill's[18] lives there, a Lawyer.

Throughout Wensleydale the Road generally runs close by the River & where that is not the case there is a foot Path which one should often take. The Inclosures all stone Walls. The People remarkably civil & obliging. Great quantities of Game of all kinds in the Valley, & on the Moors of moor Game. At Askrigg, Gyles's, the lower House, is a very good one; he knows the country well, is a very obliging honest man, & his Wife who was Mr. Pratt's Housekeeper, as himself was his Butler, cooks excellent dinners very clean & cheap.

Bainbridge a mile & $\frac{1}{4}$ from Askrigg is a small town remarkable for having been a Station[19] — Brough (hardly a Roman one from the Circumstance Aggel). On the Hill in front of it, Aggelbrough or Aid to Brough, are some Remains of fortification. Ask for Brough which is in a field near the town of Bainbridge, if you be an antiquarian.

Nappa is a Castle formerly belonging to the Metcalfes, now to Mr. Weddel, a mile from Askrigg as you go to it from Aysgarth on the left between the Road & River; the walk to it from Askrigg is a pleasant one thro' the fields, but 'tis hardly worth seeing as you have many finer Views of the Dale than from it.

The Vale of Wensley is upon the whole the most eligible one to live in & the pleasantest I ever saw. It is at the same very romantic & rustic. The Views from the tops of Middleham & Bolton Castles should never be omitted. You have also a pretty good view of the Vale from the ascent up Cam. It is said to be warmer in Winter than Parts so far north generally are, & from the Old People I saw in it I infer 'tis a very healthy Air. (However fine their seasons may be in Wensleydale, yet when I had come in the evening from Askrigg to Hawes with an intention of seeing Hardrow Scar, on a sudden the Sky overcast & it rain'd & it was dark as at Midnight in $\frac{1}{2}$ an hour. Whenever the Rain comes on in the evening this is the Case.)

Sunday 29th. 3 o'Clock.

Went from Askrigg to Ingleton 20 miles. A few miles from Askrigg you have a pretty good View of the Dale, and in one Place you catch a glimpse of Simmer Water. You then ascend for 5 miles incessantly and go on the top Ridge of a very high hill, called Cam, for about 5 more. As far as you can see, Black Moors are the only objects which present themselves to the Eye. This Road is so much exposed that by reason of the Snow it is often impassable for many days together, & the inhabitants of Askrigg and Ingleton talk of "over Cam" as if it were in a different country. The wastes though are not utterly useless since sheep are fed to the very Tops of the Mountains; near Ingleborough are very extensive Moors finely covered with Ling in which are great quantities of moor Game. Upon the very summit of Cam are several extents entirely cover'd with large Stones or rather fragments of Rock which seem to confess some great convulsion of the Earth. About 12 miles from Askrigg the Road divides and that on the left goes to Settle. Settle Rocks are discernible at 7 or 8 miles distance like rough

Eminences rudely thrown about without the least order, not very high. All the stone hereabouts will burn into Lime, & there are two Kilns just before you enter Ingleton. When I got into the Amphitheatre of Mountains I met an old man of 80 who told me the names of the Mountains. He had walked from Ingleton 8 miles and had 2 more to go, all the way uphill. On this Road you go a great way without seeing a single House. Cam Houses, 6 or 7 shabby huts, are the only ones visible for 15 or 16 miles. In the valleys is but little cultivation.

The first sight you have of Ingleborough is from ahead, grand as it breaks upon you all at once, quite clear & looking in shape like a Castle or the Side of a House. When you quit Cam you descend part of the time pretty briskly into a Valley famous in story. Before you on the left is Ingleborough, on the right Wharnside, the former 1329 Feet perpendicular height, the latter 1350 Feet. Immediately on your left is Pennygant 1310 Feet & at a distance beyond Settle Rocks is Pendle Hill, a broad clumsy large Hill 1137 Feet. Immediately on your Right is Gastill[20] & between that & Whernside at some distance by Wildbore Fells just in Westmoreland is a very black Hill, Mallerstang. The Road descends to the foot of Ingleborough and runs by the side of it for some time. About 4 miles or 3¾ from Ingleton leave the Road and go about 300 yards to the Right to see Weathercote Cave. Travel from Askrigg to Ingleton in the afternoon. It was as fine a one when I went that Road as possible and the Sun setting behind Whernside skirted the extreme Edge of the Mountain with a color the finest I ever remember to have seen, something between an Orange, a Blue, but more of a Straw color.

August 30th

Slept at Ingleton that night & spent all Monday in waiting for a Chaise to go to Settle or Hornby, in extremely bad humor in a very dirty disagreeable Inn where I had my Night Cap and Net stolen from me & the People did not seem solicitous to have them recover'd. Warrener the Master a very civil man. Walked out with him in the Afternoon to a Dell through which the River runs before it reaches the Church, & we being in a hurry did not go so far as we otherwise should have done, but I advise all People to have Time to descend to the Bottom which they can do with Ease at or near the End of the Gill. The Rocks are very high and picturesque. Go into the Church Yard & walk over the great Bridge & turn into the Meadow on your right Hand close to the River under a small wooded Hill & you have a very good View of the Town & some fields above it & of the Church which stands on an Eminence. If I recollect, you see Ingleborough too.

August 31st

On Tuesday Morning went to see Wethercote 4 miles on the Askrigg Road. (The Road over Cam very hard & indifferent.) You descend into a Cave by a very steep way but there are large holes at the Top. As you go in, large Pieces of the Rock hang over you without any visible Support and seem to threaten you with a Crush. At the end of the Cave the Rock goes up quite smooth & from the Top of it out of a Round Hole like a Mouth spouts a great stream of Water which falls for 20 yards as it is computed, I should imagine not above 10, then drops upon 2 or 3 large stones & totally disappears tho' there be no visible Hole or passage for it. The Water sounds very loud in the Cave & the Rocky sides of the Cave are petrified & look a little like the carved Stone you sometimes see at the Tops of Cathedrals. The Way into it is very indifferent in wet Weather as the Water renders the Stones very slippery. When the sun shines into the Cave, it makes the finest Rainbow in the World within it, so that it will be worth while to inquire at Ingleton at what time of the day the Sun will shine in so as to produce that beautiful Effect. Very near it is a great Hole in which in a kind of natural Well walled round by the Rock is a black dreadful-looking Water which they tell you cannot be fathom'd & it is conjectured that it has some connection with that at Wethercote. When you throw a stone in, the sound is very hollow & dreadful. Directly over Whernside about 3 miles very bad walking on the side of a Hill is a Cave called Gawder's Cave — it is also about 4 miles indifferent Road to Askrigg. In order to

42

see it you must provide yourself with plenty of candles. It goes in straight and is as wide & as high at the Entrance as in any part of it which takes off from the Effect. It is tolerably wide & high & a stream runs at the bottom, but it is hardly worth seeing as the Road to it is so very indifferent. The Cavern is above $\frac{1}{4}$ of a miles long, as the Country People informed me. They have been getting in their Harvest in every Place through which I have hitherto passed.

On Tuesday afternoon went to Hornby, north, 9 Miles. The Road is excellent & enjoyable after the bad I had travelled. (About Ingleton they fat sheep & oxen & breed some few Horses. I did not see many of the true long horn'd Craven breed but was told that they were common.) Soon after you leave Ingleton you have a Continuation of a planted eminence on the Right humble to what I had seen yet sufficiently high to be respectable, & wooded or cultivated in many Places up to the tops. Below it runs the Lune which at intervals glides peaceably along the foot of the Hills & then swells out into noble Bays. I was vastly struck with this Ride & the rich cultivated air of the country gave the Eye a great Relief after the dreary wastes of the Cam Road. The Carriage in which I went had no glass behind & it did not occur to me to look behind from the Window so that I know not whether Ingleborough could be seen though I should imagine it must be. I strolled by myself to the Castle & when I had got to the top of the rising ground Ingleborough at once broke upon my View & looked wonderfully grand & majestic.

Wednesday. Sept. 1st

Walked out in the Morning to the Castle. It is a fine old Building spoil'd by some more modern additions — it has one small Turret remaining which is discernible at a great distance. It has been in many hands. It formerly belonged to the Stanleys & is now in the Possession of a great grandson of Col. Chartres.[21] From the Top you see the Course of the River, which must have looked better a few years ago before so much Wood was cut down by its side. It is a small one & joins the Lune after a short course. I

43

believe it is only a Beck. Walk round the Castle & see the remains of greater things, but it never appears from the part which is tolerably entire to have been a place of strength except from its situation. To the North are some very extensive moors, but in general a pretty cultivated country. The River would appear to more Advantage if it did not run straight a little beyond the Castle which gives it the air of a Cut or Navigation, an Effect which the Wood must have destroyed.

From Hornby to Lancaster 9 miles. The country in general very pretty & Ingleborough commonly visible behind you. Coal Mines near the Road between Hornby & Lancaster, which are carried in little carts drawn by one Horse. About 3 miles from Lancaster opens a View the finest of the kind I ever beheld though I saw it to great disadvantage in an indifferent day & did not get the precise station. An exceedingly rich cultivated Valley in which Villages & Gentlemen's Seats are everywhere visible sufficiently to give the View an air of Population. Through it winds the Lune fringed with wood on both sides & edged with meadows at intervals. 2 planted Hills just not opposite to each other close the side near you & at the distance of 19 miles reposes Ingleborough, a complete background to the Picture, and the Interval the Mind fills up (if the Eye be not powerful enough to ascertain) with Ideas of pastoral riches, grandees and population. It is worth while to stay a day at Lancaster to see this View to advantage, which I should have done if I had not travell'd post-haste to meet Mr. Bertie. The entrance into Lancaster is found fault with: within the Town it does not at first appear to advantage, but before you enter it you have a very broad River on your Right upon whose sides runs an air of Business & (to all appearance) over it tower the Church & Castle which are fine objects. Went to the Castle, a fine building for an account of which see West.[22] The day was thick & I could but just discern the Cumberland & Westmoreland Mountains, sinking by their height Ingleborough into a Hill. Wrynose & Hardknot[23] are fine objects. Go up to the top of it & into the Churchyard where if the weather be fine you will have an excellent prospect. The Castle Yard is a very airy one.

Lancaster Church & Castle

From the drawing by Joseph Farrington from
Lakeland Views. Scenery of the Lakes, 1816

Passage House, Ulverston Sands

From the watercolour by David Cox

Thursday. Sept. 2nd

Went over the Sands to Ulverston by Cartmel & Holker, 22 miles. It is very pleasant Riding, since you are more at Liberty to look about you and less at the Road than you generally are the North Country, & nowhere is there where it answers better to gaze with all your Eyes about you. The Day brightened by degrees into a most charming one, but the Sun shone too bright to make distant objects so clear as I have sometimes known them. West's account of the Ride is a very good one. Ingleborough accompanies you to the Right for many miles, but when you see the Cumberland hills "in rude confusion hurl'd" its beauty becomes conspicuous not its sublimity. Get a Guide close to the Sands who will tell you the names of the Mountains. The sudden break into Westmoreland is wonderfully grand. At Holker is a seat of Lord G. Cavendish, who has a large Estate in the neighborhood. The People get Peats from the sides of the Hills. You come into a Theatre of them which looking wild & rude have a fine Effect. Tell the Guide to go through Holker or he will carry you a different way. There is an immense Quantity of Wood on Lord G's Estates, and the descent upon the Sands after you have ridden through the Woods is very fine. You see at a great distance some most majestic Hills & close to you is on the Right a great Bay dry at Low Water which gives you a View of the country replete with the Sublime & beautiful. If you be in a Chaise look behind you when you are about ¼ of a Mile from the Gate which goes upon the Sands. You will see the most majestic trees growing close to the Sands, & it must be delightful to walk under their cover when the Sea is up. The whole ride is a most delightful one to Ulverston; you leave the Sands 3 miles from it. A little before we left them the Tide was coming in a yard high at a great distance & the Sun shining upon it shewed like a Range of Diamonds. It has a curious appearance to see large Ships upon the dry Sand which are entirely left at low water many miles. You see on the sands many Rocks which render the navigation very dangerous. On your left the woods of Conishead Priory are visible. Upon the whole, with the natural beauties of the Country, the fineness of the day and the lively air received

46

Coniston Water

After Joseph Farington

Ambleside

From a drawing by David Cox 1816

from the Crowds of young men & maidens hurrying to & from Ulverston (pronounced Ouston) market the scene was the most delightful one I ever beheld. The Town a great one. The Inn crowded brim full of people. The land hereabouts frequently lets from about 15s. to 25s. an acre, for rather more near Hornby. From Ulverston to Ambleside 21 miles by Lowick Bridge & the edge of Hawkshead — you ride for 6 miles by the side of Coniston Lake & the Mountains at the Head of it are wonderfully sublime. You then mount a steep Hill, when turn to have a view of the Lake, rather before West directs you. You then see Esthwaite & part of Windermere but it grew dark & I went to Ambleside not enjoying the fine Scenes I might have been witness to in daylight.

Friday. Sept. 3rd

From Ambleside to Keswick 17 miles — the day so gloomy that I did not enjoy the beauties of Grasmere so much as before. The lake gives one the idea of Rasselas's happy Valley. About this country — Ambleside, Keswick etc. — when they have cut the forrest Trees the old Roots are left in the Ground which sprout out innumerable shoots and these are cut in 14 or 15 years; consequently there is little Timber, but it suits their purpose which is to make Charcoal & Posts & Rails. The View of Keswick from the Castle Rigg was not so good as 2 years ago when I saw it at sunrise, the sun illuminating the Top of the Rocks & Mountains & the Mist which the Wind drove about on the surface of the Lake with surprising Velocity. Went in the afternoon to see Mr. P's[24] House & Island, & return'd to Keswick.

Saturday. Sept. 4th

Walk'd out in the Morning intending to go but to Cockshut Hill but got beyond Lowdore which (there having been a good deal of rain the day before) was tolerably full for the summer time. Gray's[25] & West's accounts render any further description unnecessary. The former's is the best thing of the kind I ever read. Went up Cockshut Hill whence, the day being dark, the Lake did not appear to great advantage, neither is the Station so good as some others. At the entrance into Crow Park you have a fine view of Skiddaw which forms a semicircle in the right point of View, inclosing a green field gently rising just before your Eye so as to conceal the intermediate Valley; on the Left Crosthwaite Steeple is just discernible & 2 or 3 scatter'd Houses beautify the Scene as well as a small opening into the distant country. From Cockshut Hill went left-hand to come close to the North Side of the Road into Borrodale where are some inchanting Views of the Lake, every moment a new one. The closest are between Cockshut Hill & Castle Gray. You see to the Left the Lake swell'd out till it is emprison'd by the Horrid Giant of Borrodale, & the Lord's Isle & sometimes the little Round one near it are visible. You catch a Glimpse of the Water on the other side of Cockshut Hill. (After I left it the day almost immediately brighten'd & the Sun shone very bright whilst great heavy clouds sail'd swiftly along throwing upon the surrounding Hills especially Skiddaw the grandest diversity of light & shade, & veiling now one part now another of his majestic front & wrinkled seamed sides.) This directs the Eye to the Right & carries it through a beautifully cultivated Valley, where Crosthwaite & Ormathwaite etc. are capital objects till you catch the Water once more in the form of Bassenthwaite Water under a range of hills as far as the Eye can reach. It wants but a bend & swell at the end as that would besides its natural Beauty give one the Idea of its washing the far distant Hills, which are indistinctly seen beyond it. Join'd the Borrodale Road & found or thought I found West's 3rd station which I should like better if one did not look across the Water. As one walks by this side of the lake Causey Pike towers above the rest of the Hills on the other side and the little peeps into the opposite Vale are singularly beautiful. Met near Lowdore with a very civil Man who gave me some nuts, asked me to come in & take shelter from a Shower of Rain & offer'd to shew me a curious waterfall near his house. Return'd by the Borrodale Road & after dinner took a walk between Skiddaw & Keswick when a sweet innocent Girl directed me the way I should go.

Skiddaw from Applethwaite
After H. Gastineau

Sunday. Sept. 5th

The Morning rainy but I had a short walk towards the South side of the Lake. Went in the afternoon to Penrith 18 miles to see Cookson. The Road very good, the Country nothing remarkable after you leave the Environs of Keswick. The Road goes by the foot of Saddleback (so call'd from the Shape of its Top resembling that of a Saddle) a majestic mountain 3048 feet perpendicular Height; it has one or two brawny backs which look very grand & of a purple tint almost all the way up to the Top, cover'd with Ling. The tops of Cross Fell and some other high hills were shrouded in Clouds which overshadow'd too the Country beneath them; that where I was was in the Shade too for some miles whilst an intermediate space, a pretty large one, was illuminated by the Sun & contrasted with the Gloom of the other Country had a beautiful Effect. There is an old Castle of Red stone on the Right as one enters Penrith.

Monday. Sept. 6th

Left Penrith about 9 o'clock, went to Carleton, Mr. Wallace's (the Solicitor-General's) seat, & rode by the Grounds. About a mile from Penrith look directly behind you & at the End of the Lane you catch the Castle in a very picturesque manner. The country as far as Carleton except where you have Whinfell forest on the left has a very fertile appearance, & from Mr. Wallace's is a beautiful view of the country, a bird's Eye one: the River winds at the Bottom of a wellwooded & cultivated Valley & there is at a small distance a very fine Ruin, Brougham Castle. Many Hills are visible to the West & in front Cross Fell at some distance. It is certainly worth while to go this Way to or from Penrith to Keswick as it is not above a mile & ½ about at most. Rode by the side of the Eaman a clear broad River till I got into the Road, turn'd to the Left & proceeded to Keswick. Mell Fell is a remarkable Hill for it is very steep & quite Green to the very Top. Got off at a wrong place to see the Druids' Monument & wander'd about in search of it about an hour through a mistake in the maps. I fortunately met with a Traveller who told me where it was. It is in a field perhaps 50 yards distant & visible from the Road about $\frac{1}{3}$rd of a Mile from the 2 Mile stone from Keswick, nearer to it. Went upon the Water with Gisborne. Skiddaw in a Cloud look'd very majestic as it left much for the Imagination to work upon. Caught 2 or 3 Perch in the Keswick Fashion. You hold in your hands a line just over the side of the Boat & when you feel them bite you pull up. The Trout season is over though one has sometimes a few for dinner.

Tuesday September 7th

Kept in the House all day by the Rain, had some conversation with Gisborne in the morning. Hammond & Starkie arriv'd in the afternoon.

Wednesday September 8th

Set out in the Morning with Hammond, Starkie & Gisborne under the Conduct of Tom Hutton. Went in the Borrodale Road till we came to Barrow Gill, about 2 miles & $\frac{1}{2}$ from Keswick at Noton House where we dismounted & proceeded up the Hill on the Left. It is a Waterfall well worth seeing. The Water has worn its way through the solid Rock & has in one Place formed a Bason in it which is very deep & called the Prison from the impossibility there would be that a person put in could escape out of it. Near it is another Waterfall, called Catgill, but we were told there was then no water in it. Proceed about 200 yards till you come to a Gate but instead of going through it turn to the Left where the Road leads up a Hill, Barrowside (the Hill whence Barrow Gill falls), in the Road to Ashness & Watenlath, the latter of which about 3 miles off is a Tarn on the Top of a Hill which feeds Lowdore & a small village of the name. It is a bad road to it over the Mountains. A little before you reach the 1st Gate in going up the Hill is a kind of Flat by the side of the Road where is one of the finest general Views of the Lake I ever saw. Another not quite so good an one but where you have a sight of Lowdore & Borrodale is higher up just beyond the 2nd

Gate. These should never be omitted. But if you content yourself with going round the Lake once, without reversing that Round, you should turn about every moment that you may comprehend all the Beauties of this singular Place, Beauties which are changing every step you take.

Return'd to the Road the same way we came, & proceeded to Lowdore, which was tolerably full. The sun shone very bright & the scene was beautiful beyond description. To see it properly you must not content yourself with West's station, but get down to the bed of the Waterfall, which you may very easily a little above to the Left. Its appearance is then much more wonderful. The Rock on the Left, Gowder Crag, is finer for the purpose than Salvator[26] could have given; that on the Right, Shepherds Crag. The Chasm is narrow & in the Morning when you look up it is fine to see the Clouds sailing above you & the Sun illuminating the Top & foam of the Water when you yourself are in the Shade. Look back upon the Lake & Mountains. On the Right, from behind a piece of Rock which projected, breasted forth a Torrent of Water which I caught in my Glass[27] (through a tree romantically fix'd in the Bare Rock & twisted) shining like diamonds, a Picture the finest my eyes ever beheld. Very little of this can be seen without descending, & by varying your station & going to all Parts you will discover new & unparallel'd Beauties. Consider'd as a Waterfall I have seen superior, but taking in the accompaniments, the immense Rock on the Left steep as a Castle Wall & whiter than they generally are in this Country, seen sometimes bare, sometimes through Trees fantastically disposed, with the back View of the Lake, never could such a scene enter into the Imagination of Man to conceive. The fall is not a perpendicular one but the Rocks or Stones which prevent its being so it has by its own Violence strewed the way with, & it leaps over them with irresistible fury. They are sometimes all covered when it is said that the very Earth shakes beneath you. It was with the utmost regret I quitted this most enchanting Scene. Before you go up on the left see a little perpendicular fall on the Right of the Mill.

Went up Borrodale by Grange Bridge, some fine pointed Rocks on the left. Came to the Bowder Stone, the River all

The Bowder Stone & Castle Crag
After Joseph Farington

Derwentwater & Valley of Grange
from the entrance to Borrowdale
After Thomas Allom

the time bearing you company. It answers to get off & look
under it. It stands upon a Ridge almost as small as the
Keel of a Ship. Went up near Seathwaite & saw the
Mountains Great Gavel[28] & Great End which shut up the
mouth of Borrodale. On the left in a hollow of Glaramara
rather before you reach it is Eagle Crag, from the
Circumstance of there being an Eagle's nest there. They lay
two eggs once every year. West's account of the taking of
the young is strictly true. Bull Crag, another of the Rocks
on the left before Eagle Crag, is so called because the Eccho
is there so great & so often repeated that a Bull can never
be held there long, above 2 years old, without going mad
from hearing the Returns of its own roarings. I have heard
of the same Thing happening in other mountainous
Countries. Above Seathwaite (the 2nd Village beyond
Bowder, Rosthwaite 1st), on the top of the Hill, is the
Wadd Mine.[29] It was open'd last year when from their
having taken out a double Quantity it is reckon'd they have
enough for the Consumption of 20 years. It will sometimes
sell for 25 or 30s. a lib. or 18 or 20s. a lib. The hole was
formerly fill'd up with stones & rubbish, the removal of
which when it was last open'd is said to have cost £300. It
is now fill'd up with Water except just at the Top which
they can instantly remove by a Level made into the Side of
the Hill, at little Trouble or Expence.

Return'd to Grange, saw the young farmer where Gray
was so civilly receiv'd, his name Caleb Fisher.[30] The Rocks
opposite Grange look rudely thrown together. The View
into Borrodale finer than from the other Side of the Lake
about $\frac{1}{2}$ or $\frac{3}{4}$ of a mile from Grange. The surprizing Blueness
of the Water will or ought to strike very much. Saw the
Tracks down which come the Sledges loaded with Turf.
They are very small & in the steepest places. The sledges
are without wheels and have 2 long Handles which the
Man takes hold of. To his Heels are spikes fix'd & to the
Front of the Sled against which he leans his Rump is a
Cushion. Glaramara a most surprizing Extent of bare Rock,
which is broken in a wonderful manner like little hills upon
a great Carpet of Rock. Not far from Grange in the Side of
the Hill are several Holes made in expectation of finding
Lead Mines, none have been found. Return'd home through

Portingscale & by Crossthaite Church.

Went in the Evening after dinner in the Boat to Swinside from whence is a fine View of the Vales of Newlands & Keswick. They looked like a Carpet under one, divided in all shapes & by all colors. The Hedge Rows (not a stone Wall in sight) are all mix'd with Trees in them. Bassenthwaite, for we saw it from one End to the other in a straight Line, looked like a ditch. But the Afternoon was a very indifferent one & none of its wooded sides are thence visible. Under Swinside a curious Hill, a sandy color tufted with green Tufts, looked just like a great piece of spotted Cloth thrown over the Hill. To the best of my Recollection it is in Foe Park;[31] Foe Park is under Swinside.

Thursday September 9th

Set out between 7 & 8 with Gisborne & Tom Hutton, to Buttermere. Passed thro' Portingscale & through the delightful Vale of Newlands. The Vale becomes less smiling as you proceed, till you come to where it appears to close up, the Hills on each Side & those in front very high. In your way to this place you have a very fine View of Catbells, Lady's Bower[32] etc., viewing them on the Side contrary to that which you see from the Lake. The Passage through the Mountains where it appears to be clos'd up is called Newlands Hawse. On the Left is a Waterfall & a little Bason in the Rock from whence it is fed. In front a very great Waterfall. Go through the Hawse & you have a most striking Scene of Wildness & Desolation. A new collection of Mountains surrounds you. This road has been improv'd since West's Account. Before you reach Buttermere you see a very great Waterfall pouring down from one of the Hills which is near the Lake. When we got to the Ale House we went to the left by the Side of Buttermere, dismounted & walk'd close to the Water. The Lake is a small one & the Mountains rise directly from the Lake as Perpendicular as a Wall, & of an immense height opposite to them are very high Rocks not close to the Water. The Road to the left proceeds into Borrodale by Honistar Crag and the Wadd mine.

Return'd & went through the village of Buttermere.

Buttermere

After Thomas Allom

Crummock Water

After Thomas Allom

(Goose Gate[33] is a Right of putting & fatting two geese on the common, Whittle Gate is a right of dining with his parishioners by turns every Sunday, Harden Sark such as the Carters use & clog & two strong Shoes annually.) The lake of Buttermere one of the most savage ones I saw. It has Char in it & fine Trout. To Crummock water, took a Boat across the Head of the Lake & proceeded on foot by the side of it a little way; went about $\frac{1}{2}$ a mile up on the Left just before we came to Mellbreack to see a Waterfall. There is a Stone Wall which will carry a stranger to it. It is in a Cleft of the Rock about 2 or 3 or 4 yds. over, & it falls perpendicular about 30 yards as I imagine, the Country People say much more. After it has fallen it proceeds in the Cleft about 20 or 30 yds. where it falls for 10 or 12 feet into the open Valley. To see it properly climb up beyond the first fall. Whilst we were there it grew so thick that we could scarce see across the Lake & a drizzly rain fell so that we could just discern Grassmire a vast red Hill standing opposite Mellbreak. They look like guards on each side of the Lake. Went to Scale Hill, got some Eggs & Bacon & rode home. The Vales of Lorton and Brackenthwaite were seen to a sad disadvantage. Came into the Whinlater Road at the 6th Mile Stone. Saw Bassenthwaite below us on the left.

Friday September 10th

Got up betwixt 5 & 6 & attempted to scale Skiddaw whose Top was quite clear when we (Mr. Hutton & myself) set off. Rode to the Bottom of the Hill & there left our Horses. After having ascended about as high as Latrigg, the steepest part of the Climb, the day overcast & clouds entirely covered over $\frac{1}{2}$ of the Mountain. We staid, in hopes of the day mending, an hour, when we came down giving up all Expectation of a fine day. On a sudden it brighten'd up & we set forward a 2nd time, & were again turn'd back, so that we determined to be fool'd no longer & to give up the Scheme. Our Labor however upon the whole was well rewarded, as from the Side of the Hill we saw the most Beautiful Scenes. When we began to ascend the 1st Time the Sun shone upon the Lake which was as blue as the Sky

58

& as unruffled as a Looking Glass. The Vale of Keswick look'd beautiful beyond description, the peaceful retreat of some favor'd Mortals undisturb'd by the Cares & Concerns of the World. There was but just wind sufficient to agitate the light vapor which sometimes dropped upon the Ground, & then was gently rais'd up again. The Village dogs bark'd, the Partridge call'd & all was rural Peace & pastoral Enjoyment. Presently the vapor thicken'd and spread by degrees from the opening into Borrodale, till it entirely surrounded us so thick that we could not see even to the Bottom of the Mountain. On a sudden in 4 or 5 minutes at the most it was below quite clear again (Nature's Curtain drew up & discover'd a most wonderful scene) & it look'd like the darkness of Chaos rolling off & bringing to light a New Creation. Such a scene my Eyes never beheld. Dr. Brownrigg's[34] House a pleasing object. The inclination of the Mountain (foreshortening it) made the Cornfields & Meadows at its Bottom appear close to me & serve as a fore ground to the Rest of the Prospect. The opening into Newlands Vale was very fine and induc'd one to think that there were other such retreats concealed amongst the other Mountains which we saw towering as far as the Eye could see.

Went upon the Lake about 12 o'clock with Cookson & Farrington.[35] It was perfectly calm & the Mountains, Rocks & Trees etc. were reflected so perfectly on the Water that one could have discern'd in the Reflection the smallest object & in the Glass (which answer'd delightfully) it was difficult to say which was the Shadow and which the Reality. The Ecchoes were vastly fine & repeated like Thunder after one had imagined them lost. Went to Lowdore which was not so full as before, so that there was not that breasting of the Water. From thence walk'd through Grange to Castle Hill, which we ascended without much difficulty. The best way of going up is by the Way which they bring the Slate, to which anyone at Grange will direct you, a very good walking way. The View from it was the most striking I saw at Keswick. An immense Rock on your Left, another near as high on your Right look like Giants to support Castle Hill the Champion of Borrodale. From it you see under you a beautiful little Vale, water'd by the River (which tho' in some parts beautifully winding is hardly large enough for the Purpose). The Prospect is there quite a Bird's Eye one, & ends in two little dells that appear to go in amongst the Mountains. Under you to the north east is the Village Bridge of Grange & beyond there is the inclosure & river, & over the Lake the most surprizing object of all, Skiddaw, who look'd quite different from what I ever saw him before or since. The sun shone upon every part of it & it look'd like the smiling King which West compares it to. It was spread out in a most wonderful manner so as to form a complete Back Ground, & look'd like the hundred-handed Giant Briareus.[36] On our way back look'd in about Grange upon an extraordinarily sequester'd Scene. There was a green field almost encircled by Mountains. 'Tis on the left Hand & a Gate opens from it into a narrow Lane just before, as I believe, you come to another Gate in the Lane. From Lowdore to Keswick by water. The Islands do not look well from Castle Hill being too near the other End of the Lake. The best situation of viewing them is from the ascent up Skiddaw.

Saturday September 11th

Set out in the morning to ride round Bassenthwaite, the Road to Ewsbridge,[37] 9 miles, lies under Skiddaw which does not look so grand as from Keswick. About 5 or 6 miles there is a wooded Hill, I think Wildthorpe,[38] & a great stretch of the Water in length and a Bend at the end. It soon began to rain & was thick all the Time. Went round the other side, bad road, return'd to Keswick, din'd with Mr. Farrington.

Sunday September 12th

Went to Church in the Morning & heard an excellent Sermon. After Church took a snack & went up Skiddaw. When we had got about $\frac{1}{2}$ way to the Top, the day grew thick & was never fine afterwards throughout; it was quite clear almost all round except into Borrodale etc. by little slips at a Time. The Sun shone very bright upon the Sea, upon which 6 or 7 Ships were seen quite plain with the naked Eye. The View into Northumberland & Scotland is very extensive. The Isle of Man is very visible. You see the Caldew from its rise 100 yds. below you to where it falls into the Sea & makes the Solway Firth. You see a Hill which is said by the Guide to be near Newcastle, & some hills are seen to the North which may perhaps be 90 or 100 miles off. The Country to the North is a very fine one, that to the East not so good. Brougham Castle looks 3 or 4 miles off, in reality 18. Scruffel[39] in Scotland attracts one's notice, & I do not wonder that the country people made them acquainted, as there is no rising ground betwixt them. Skiddaw is parted from Saddleback by a little brook, Glenderaterra, & comprehends several hill-lings, in all I should imagine not less at its base than 20 or 30 miles round. Mr. Graham's House just in Scotland is a pretty object, & the View is far greater than I could have suppos'd & the objects seen much more distinctly. Carlisle, lying low, is not visible. The Air is very cold at the Top, & the wind almost always very high. Upon it are two Heaps of Stones, upon which people who go generally write their names, which are upon a ridge, narrow, at the very Top of the Mountain. On the East side of this, the coldest, some most curious Plants & Mosses grow on a little Earth between the Stones of which the side is compos'd for a considerable way. The Ridge runs nearly north & south. Under you Bassenthwaite water & another lake (& upon the top of a Hill to the right a little Bason of Water) make appearance. One may go up on Horseback the greater Part of the Way, as there are no stones till you get almost to the Summit, & between the different Tops, on the Part that looks like the Seat of a little Saddle, is a mile & $\frac{1}{2}$ good riding. There is no forming any Idea of the Height (Crossfell is blue, rises gradually & is very distinctly seen closing the Prospect 26 miles off to the East) of this stupendous mountain without ascending it & seeing the Difference there is between the Heights of the several Points which look from below to be almost all upon a level.

They who have never been upon the Top of a very high Mountain cannot conceive that it is possible for Brydone's[40] account to be not much exaggerated. The Vales of Keswick, Bassenthwaite & Newlands look like a Map or the Plan of

Brougham Castle
From Francis Grose's *Antiquities*

Keswick from Greta Bridge
After H. Gastineau

an Estate with their different enclosures of a like size to those. (It is too high to see the Lake etc.) Walla Crag and the other Rocks look humble, & Latrigg under your feet looks a green field not above the level of the ground, & half way down the Mountain you can just perceive that it rises. Its Top is perfectly green & has a beautiful appearance; compare it to a Woman or a green Cushion. I am at a loss to account for the appearance of the Sea which at the end of the Horizon look'd as high or higher than we were. In this country the clouds often collect in vast masses at a distance, generally over the Sea, blue or dark, & put on the appearance of Mountains, Rocks, Fields, etc.; behind them the sun sets, & looks better than retiring behind the Hills for the Edges of the Cloud look jagged like those of the Inside of the Crescent[41] through any Telescope: red, yellow & all colors. Such a sun was setting, by much the finest I ever beheld. Sheep feed almost to the top of Skiddaw. Goats are not kept in this country because the sheep following them would tumble down the Precipices. The Shepherds have known the snow between the Gills of Skiddaw 100 yards drift. From the Top we saw a canopy of Cloud sailing over the Sea at a little distance which wild & hairy — like Eyebrows — stream'd like a Meteor. To the Top from the foot it is reckon'd 4 miles, from Keswick $5\frac{1}{2}$ or 6.

September 13th

Monday morning a very bad one. Went a little way round Latrigg & he bullied us. Went up part of him where steepest. Return'd over the Wood bridge by the Penrith Road, din'd, drank Tea with Farrington & Miss Wood & supp'd at Home with Haggard, Sumner etc.

Tuesday September 14th

Cookson went to Cockermouth. When I was going in the morning to Wyburn water my Horse prov'd lame. Order'd him back & walk'd to the Bridge over the Greta on the Penrith Road $\frac{1}{2}$ a mile. The Bridge is safe tho' not pleasant. When over got into a Green Road that goes round at the foot sometimes at the Ankle of Lattrigg & it is an easy

Lowdore Cataract
After Thomas Allom

Walk which I would have every body take that comes to Keswick. It may be done in the ascent up Skiddaw, sending their horses to meet them by the Ormathwaite side of Latrigg. Though the day was not perfectly fine, rather thick towards Borrodale, I have scarcely seen a pleasanter scene. You look down upon the Vale of Keswick, on the south see the Vale of St. John's, Helvellyn, & the river Greta winding its way to the Town, which looks beautiful, as well as Crosthwaite Church, the Prospect a Bird's Eye one. Walking on you break at once upon Skiddaw & most majestic & portly does he shew. Look upon the Right, Bassenthwaite Water is seen with Dr. B.'s white House under you & several cottages dispos'd along the Vale. The Rocks of Borrodale to be view'd through a Glass. Wallow Crag etc. very fine. Lowdore Falls. Castle Hill & Cockshut Hill & an Island seen betwixt them. The Vale of Newlands on each side of Swinside. Ten thousand different Inclosures & Trees in the Hedge Rows. Went up Latrigg on the Side opposite Dr. B.'s & walk'd on till I saw the turns & windings of the River which West speaks of, but not going the same way could not find his exact Stations. Cross Fell blue & gently sloping. St. John's & Helvellyn. It began to rain very fast & I was wet to Skin before I reach'd Keswick. Instead of going with Mr. F. to Ormathwaite confin'd to the House all night by the Wet. (N.B. In all our Rides by it we stopp'd for a minute at the Horseing Stone at the Vicarage.)[42]

Wednesday September 15th

Went in the morning to the Vicarage Garden. The view sweetly pastoral & the Church tho' new a fine object. It rises as venerable as is consistent with simplicity & humility. The owner of the Living lives at Bottisham. Hop'd the day would turn out well & set out for Cockermouth, in my way to see Bassenthwaite, 16 miles. About 6 miles from Keswick turn'd down to Scareness, a wooded promontory. It began to rain fast & grew so thick that I could not see across the Lake. Bradness we pass'd in our way to Scareness. Unable to see anything we got into the Road again a ¾ of a mile before Ewsbridge. A great Hill breasts into the Water very finely near Ewsbridge (opposite Armathwaite) which returns a Bar of Music like that at Middleham.[43] The Landlord a very civil obliging man. From Old Park above Armathwaite is said to be a very fine view of the Lake & Derwent Water & Borrodale. Rode in the Rain to the Globe at Cockermouth over a dreadful Moor the greater part of the way. Saw Whinlater on the Left. Had Cookson for Supper & a very good Bed. Walk'd to the Castle & heard the Derwent roar.

Thursday September 16th

Bad unpromising day, so took a Chaise & went to Whitehaven, 14 miles. (On the Castle Hill great Quantities of Slate have been got for many years, & in digging for it much freestone is found of various colors, though there is no other freestone to be had within 20 miles. They find Stones too sometimes cut into a kind of Trough in which the Country Man told me it was conjectur'd the Romans used to feed their Fowls.) The country between Cockermouth & Whitehaven not very good. About four miles from Cockermouth are 3 or 4 Coal Mines which have been work'd many years & 2 Steam Engines. You see the Sea many miles before you reach Whitehaven. It is the best built seaport I ever saw. The Streets run in general at right angles & the Houses uniform, though from the Collieries & Smoke they are rather black. It was built not above 100 years ago. It lies in a Bottom between two hills, which shelter it from the North & South, & I think there is another which protects it from the East. From the West Wind the Ships are shelter'd by six long Piers which stretching in different directions break the force of the Waves. Against them the Ships are moor'd. On them they lade & unlade their goods & there are holes through some of them, like small Arches of a Bridge, by which Boats go from one of the six little Harbors to another without going round the Pier. The Ships all entirely dry at low Water. A few large Cannon are on a Battery on the South West of the Town near the Sea Side & a few more, with Turf Embrasures lately made, at a place dignified by the name of Garrison, a force seemingly inadequate[44] to the defence of

Cockermouth Castle
From Francis Grose's *Antiquities*

Whitehaven
After G. Pickering

the place.

The Trade is chiefly confin'd to Ireland & the Isle of Man (which is distinctly visible from the Seashore). Coals are the Chief Article of Exportation. They had formerly a great trade to Virginia & Maryland but since that is stopp'd the Vessels are chiefly gone into the Transport Service & you see few large ones in the Harbor. The Isle of Man is a bold hilly Object with an invisible neck of Land that connects it with another mountainous Shore, the Calf of Man. St. Bees Head a fine black Rock to the South, which serves the Sailors as a land mark. The Scotch Hills and Shore rounding at the End of Cumberland make an immense Bay that has a grand Appearance. But the great Support of Whitehaven is its Coal Mines, chiefly the property of Sir James Lowther, who it is imagined gets an annual clear income of £18,000 from them. They are some of them close to the Town, others near two miles off. Mr. Lutwidge[45] not being at home when I call'd I could get but little intelligence respecting them (or the Trade). They are very strict about shewing them & the Overseer, Mr. Spedding, they told me at the Inn, denied Ld. Wensley & Mr. Granville the Week before I was there.

The Coal is not found in Veins but in a kind of stratum or layer extending far and wide. They leave pillars of coal to support the incumbent Earth, & when they can find little they thin these, & when they quit the Mine almost entirely take them away, which is call'd robbing the mine. (A great number of fathoms of solid Rock, suppos'd so firm as not to be in any danger of falling in, did, so necessary are these Pillars. I think it was near Newcastle.) The Works under Ground are very extensive & are carried a great Way under the Sea. Their Caution about shewing them is perhaps occasion'd by their fears of their being set on fire. They in general find the Coal by boring to a great depth, perpendicularly. Sometimes it rises from below on an inclin'd Plane, so that you can go in with Ease. The Place where it opens in this Way is call'd the Beer or Bear Mouth. The Shafts are very long & the miners who are let down in Buckets are in danger for the smallest Stone falling on their Heads might do them a material Injury falling from such a Height. The Common Mark of Coal beneath is a dirty, blackish, crumbling Soil on a freestone, or some kind of stone. They are greatly subject to Damps in these Mines, especially the fire damp, so that in some of them the Light they receive is from a Wheel full of flints turning against a Steel, as flame not sparks sets the damp on fire. The most dangerous & unwholesome time of visiting them, a Physician told me, was in the Autumn or latter end of Summer. There is a Steam Engine. They meet sometimes with a strong demonstration of some deluge or internal convulsion of the Earth — Coal, Stone, Earth & all kinds of Soil strangely jumbled & thrown together all at once in a bed of Coal, which upon removing that is found as before.

The Coal is raised out of the Mines by a Horse & put into Waggons which hold I forget the exact Quantity but I am sure $\frac{1}{2}$ a ton. These have Wheels of cast Metal, & there are Roads made on purpose for them on the South Hill where it overlooks the Town, which have an inclination from the Mine to the Town, & have a piece of Wood on each side (sometimes two abreast) that exactly fits the Wheels so that the Carriages can in most places be push'd by men. These Roads terminate in a large Warehouse from which there are six Great funnels which go at the Bottom into the Holds of the Ships & the Bottom of the Cart lets the Coals into it at the Top. The funnels are called Hurries. They have a contrivance to prevent the Waggons going too quick, a piece of iron, I think, pressing upon the Wheels. Lest there should not be ships ready to receive the Coal, there is another Floor, beneath, of the same Warehouse, in which it is dropped in the same manner as in the Hurries & in which it lays till there be a demand for it. There is a contrivance for the Waggon to go from one Part of the Warehouse to another: at the Place where the different Roads meet there is a Part of the floor large enough to receive the Waggon which turns upon a Pivot & 2 men can with Ease (sometimes one does it) turn that round till it comes in a line with the Way they mean to go. There are many of them as there is by means of them a communication through all that floor of the Warehouse to the 6 different Hurries. The Road in the Warehouse is fitted with Wood in the same manner except that it is shod with Iron. One Horse draws the Waggons back to the mouth of the mine, & sometimes from it where there is a difficult place. The Wheels of the Waggons are made like a Groove, but are as if one side of the Groove was taken away, that on the outside of the Wheel. Sir James Lowther's Place[46] at the flats has cost him an immense sum of money & there are many entertaining stories relative to it which are told in the neighborhood. Return'd to Cockermouth at night.

Friday September 17th

After raining all the night before it still continu'd to rain & was a dreadful day. Played a game at Billiards in the morning. Cookson din'd out, supp'd with me & Mr. Lothian. Confin'd to the House all day by the Rain. Walk'd out to the Castle which looks very well from the Bridge. It is entirely in Ruins & has been a strong one; it is surrounded on one side by the Cocker & on the other by the Derwent, which join almost under its Walls. There is a kind of Vault below where is an immense weight of Building all resting upon a single Arch. Skiddaw & all the Mountains veil'd in Clouds. A pretty Village to the North a mile off, seen through an old Window.

Saturday September 18th

Thought of setting out in the Morning, when there came on a most violent storm of Wind & Rain with thunder & lightning. (A man was once shot dead from the Castle at a place which must be near ¾ of a mile off.) Cookson & I in the afternoon took a Ride as far as the end of Crummock Water & walk'd up (according to West's direction) above Mr. Bertie's Woods. The View is of a very fine valley water'd by the Cocker which appear'd to great advantage from having overflow'd its Banks & made new swells & bends. West's description of the View is very exact & good. Grasmire frowns awfully behind on the Left & Mellbreak on the Right. A pretty View of that side of Crummock & the valley between it & Loweswater, part of which is visible. While we were out were 2 Violent Storms of Rain & Hail but we luckily took Shelter in Scale Inn. We had not time to go to the House West speaks of by the Gate leading

Ennerdale
After Thomas Allom

Loweswater
After Thomas Allom

to Ennerdale. It was dark before we reached Cockermouth & the wind cold and uncomfortable. The Ride about 15 miles.

Sunday September 19th

The morning as usual rainy & cold. Towards 12 o'Clock it brighten'd up & weary of being so long confin'd to an Inn I set off about 2 to go by Ennerdale to Holm Rook. I took a Guide with me to Ennerdale Bridge. It rain'd soon after I set out until I got there. The country for some miles near Cockermouth very bad, an extended moor with high mountains at some distance to close the Scene. About six miles off there are marks of cultivation all the way to Ennerdale Bridge, but the country poor. You pass a small tarn, Ullock Tarn, in which are many Trout, & leave Mockerkin on a Hill on the left. Went from the Public House at Ennerdale Bridge to How Hill, 1 mile & $\frac{1}{2}$, to have a View of the Water. It is surrounded 3 ways by high Mountains, its sides are some of them interspers'd with self-planted Wood. You see a great Mountain before you call'd Pillar. How Hall the country people said was a very old Place, in the time of the Romans they thought, & many Images etc. had been found in it. As one stands on the Hill the shape of the Lake is not much unlike that of England. It is said to be 4 miles long & 1 over — I should not think it so much. A Rock or two on the North West come close to the Water Edge, & there is a little Rocky something, an Island, peeping out of the Water. There are Char in it, which about Michaelmas come into the River which runs out of the Lake, & lie in Shoals upon the Sand or Gravel. They are never caught in the Summer except one by Chance. I saw the Lake, 'tis true, to a disadvantage but in my Opinion it is not worth going far out of one's way to see. The Whitehaven people (it is 7 or 8 miles off) often come to fish there. The Vale is a large one & is said to be very healthy; my Guide pointed me out a House where liv'd a Man ag'd 100. They had several in the Parish nearly of a like age, and said that his ancestors for some generations had not died younger.

From Ennerdale Bridge to Calder Bridge 6 miles over a

Hill call'd Cold Fell. One has from it a fine View of the Sea & the Isle of Man. I saw something in my Glass, I fancy it must have been the Hills on the far side of the Isle of Man, which I took at first for Ireland. There was a most Heavenly Sun setting, something of the same kind with what I saw in my descent from Skiddaw, except that below the dark blue Clouds a piece of red sky came in & redden'd the Sea at the End of the Horizon & went in one Part as they paint Rain. I stay'd long looking at it & did not reach Calder Bridge till after Sunset, where hearing Mr. Lutwidge was not at Home I took up my quarters all Night & had a tolerable Bed.

Monday September 20th

Walk'd in the morning to see the Ruins of Calder Abbey. There is nothing very striking in them. The Building seems to have been a large one from the four large arches which seem to have been the Middle or entrance to three sides behind each of which there must have been as much as there is now behind one of them. That which remains is in general low yet venerable from being cover'd with Ivy. Between it and the River stands a white House, Mr Senhouse, opposite to which on a steep hill on the other side of the River is a great Quantity of Wood. It would mend the View much if the Abbey were amongst the Trees on the other side, or the Hill not so steep & the House upon its declivity, the Trees on it being remov'd toward where the Abbey stands at present.

Went by Santon Bridge over the Irt which comes out of Wast Water & falls into the sea at Ravenglass. Into Wastdale. You have on the Way a good view of the Sea & Isle of Man & the Elbow'd Harbor of Ravenglass which was once a great Place but now though it has a market consists of a very few Houses. Before you reach Santon Bridge you see a high Hill with a kind of crack in it. This is Sca Fell said by the People thereabouts to be higher than Skiddaw. As you enter Wastdale the Appearance is very striking. You are in a great Valley almost completely skirted and ringed by Rocks of an immense Height & at the End you see one in the Styehead like the sharpest part of a

Wedge which closes the whole. It seems as if it were design'd to be floated by some immense Lake. Wastwater is far too inconsiderable for the Purpose. You presently come to it after passing by two or three small Houses. It is a narrow Lake without any Wood or Cultivation at its Banks except a little at its outlet on the West End. An immense Rock Scree runs by the south side of it the whole Length, whose sides where they are not directly perpendicular are cover'd with Shivers[47] amongst which one sees vast fragments of Rock that have tumbled from the Top. The place has a most savage Appearance. On the left a little behind is a Rock steep as a Wall & the Inclosures of this Extraordinary Vale are all Rocks not Hills. Wastwater is 4 miles long & I should guess hardly $\frac{1}{2}$ a one broad, tho' they tell you 'tis one. You ride by the side of it its whole length when the dale narrows and there fronts you a curious Rock just the Shape of the Brink of Strombolo or Mount Vesuvius. You may almost stride over the Top of it though high. On the Right is Sca Fell. Saw two country men driving sheep, observing their Shoes more clumsy than the clumsy ones of the Country I ask'd their Weight & he told me betwixt 7 & 8 but that he had a pair at Home which weigh'd 9 pounds.

Take a Guide at Wastdale Head to lead you into Borrodale. All the scenery is the most barren & desolate imaginable. There runs a Brook which divides Great End & Gavel, the outposts of Borrodale, the first on the Right the other on the left. The Road here becomes dreadfully bad & that it may get up the Hill winds in a most extraordinary manner. This goes on to the End. But the better way of going is letting your Horses be led & walking in the foot Path over the Gavel. You have from it a View of the Sea as if from between two Walls & of the Valley of Wastdale. The Mountain itself looks dreadful as it stands bristling up in spiked columns above the Shivers & Ruins which it has made. It is reckon'd dangerous passing over in a frost, as the Rock then cracks & rolls violently down in huge fragments. From the Ascent you have a clear View of the Windings of the other Road. When you get to the Top there is a small Valley in which there is a Lake perhaps $\frac{3}{4}$ of a Mile round call'd Styehead Tarn. There are many Trout in

Wastwater
After Thomas Allom

Wastdale Head
After Thomas Allom

it, but far more in another on the other side of Great End, call'd Sprinkling — in the maps Sparkling — Tarn. You have then a View of Helvellyn, something similar to that of Skiddaw from Castle Hill, or of the Sea from the Ascent except that it looks far higher than you. You see on the Left a Hill with some little grass upon it which Peculiarity is reckon'd a sufficient distinction from the other Hills of the Place & it is accordingly called Green Gavel.

You soon begin to descend into Borrodale, & its green fields & Inclosures give a most agreeable Relief to the Eye after the Barrenness & Rudeness which have hitherto engross'd it. As you go down Glaramara is on the Right next to End,[48] not where the Guide informs you, & the Wadd Hill on your Left at some distance. My Guide was a very civil obliging man. His name John Braithwaite or Thomas Braithwaite of Wastdale Head. I conjectur'd that the water could not descend from so great a Height into Borrodale without some Waterfall. My Guide accordingly conducted me to a very fine one, & with much difficulty I got close to it. It is (as you go up Borrodale from Keswick) about $\frac{3}{4}$ of a mile from Seathwaite, on the Right at the End of the dale. The Water falls perpendicularly over a black marble a considerable Height, I should think 20 yards or more (they say many more). On the left are Trees rudely dispos'd among the naked Rock which 50 or 100 or 200 yds. from the fall rises gradually to the Place whence the Water falls. On the Right at some little distance is Force Crag, one of the same kind but I thought at the time finer than Falcon Crag, more shining, & rising gradually as the other. I frequently ask'd the Names of the Mountains about Wastdale & the Stye Head, some of which I set down. I find a list of barbarous Names — Yewbarrow, Hind Crag, Heedderland Fell, Gavel, End, Green Gavel, Seat, Kirk Fell, Taylor Gill (a Taylor was once demolish'd there) etc., etc. The name of the Waterfall is I think Green How (Hill) Force. A fine Waterfall just above Seathwaite to the left going to Keswick.

It was a delightful Evening & I saw innumerable new Beauties in Borrodale. When the Sky has that clearness which it has in a Summer or rather Autumnal Evening the Mountains appear to stand off in a particular Manner (perhaps the Contrast of the whitish Blue) which I cannot adequately describe, but the Effect of which every one must have perceived. I can compare it to the standing off of the Clouds when view'd in the convex Mirror. There is no dazzle, all is distinctness & the Outline clearly defin'd. Castle Hill had that Appearance, & I never saw anything more beautiful than it look'd flanked by those two immense Rocks, that on the South East a particularly fine one, from a kind of great Pillow or Pasty of Rock in a Line betwixt it & Skiddaw a little way from it. From this Pasty the River too was visible. As you proceed new Wonders strike you & I made & pencill'd down several observations of Beauties that I had not before remark'd, but unfortunately the Pencil mark wore out in my Pocket & disappeared. Before you reach Lowdore, you come into a Bay of Rocks, that are very fine, near which are some like the Matlock Rocks, white & with Trees. Castle Rock stands boldly forward jutting his Head that looks at the same Time venerable & amiable. It is black from underwood & its head set upon another Hill, a pair of shoulders, 'tis like a Dog on his Backside.

I had often heard of the Effect of the Moonshine & the Waterfalls at night & the Lake, & I accordingly sent word from Castle Rock to dispatch Hutton to me. I in the meantime went in a small Boat upon the Lake. The Moon shone very bright but did not look near so fine as at Sea. The Waterfalls sounded dreadfull. It grew dark, windy, & they missing me, I was very near spending the Night upon the Lake. I found little Cookson at the Inn & fell asleep in my Chair as soon as Supper was over in spite of all my Endeavors, so went off to Bed.

The Road I came that day a most extraordinary one. Wildness & desolation the more prevailing features. The Lake at the Top had neither wood nor cultivated fields nor Houses about it. Cockermouth is a pretty large place, though not I suppose above $\frac{1}{3}$ of the size of Whitehaven, consisting chiefly of one very large wide street. The Inhabitants are reckon'd to be about 3000 or perhaps more, the Shalloons[49] are the only articles of manufactory; the Place was much more populous (5000) before the commencement of the American Disputes, when there were a prodigious Quantity of Hats exported. It is not, I am told, a very healthy Place. The Borough is absolutely Sir James Lowther's. There are about 200 Voters — Burgage Tenures[50] which he has secure to him.

Tuesday September 21st

An unpleasant morning & my horse lame. Walk'd out to Cockshut Hill in the middle of the day. I cannot say that this View of the Lake pleases me so well as many others. One of the prettiest Objects (besides Wallow Crag & those seen from all parts of the Lake) is a delightful green Peninsula with a House & Trees on it which forms a sweet Bay on the other side under Walla Crag opposite the Lord's Island. The Views of Keswick & Skiddaw are very good between Cockshut Hill & the Town. Crow Park is not at all a favorite Station with me. The Weather soon grew bad & prognosticated a coming Storm from which I fled home & by which I was prevented all night from visiting Mr. Farrington.

Wednesday September 22nd

The Day promis'd for some time to be no better than the preceding ones, but I ventur'd forth & it grew tolerably good. Pass'd Cut Gill & Barrow Gill & reach'd Lowdore in a very decent fall. It is in an awful Chasm form'd between two immense Rocks, that on the Right black & white yet shining with the Rain with Trees here & there fantastically dispos'd, that on the left higher than the other, naked & rounded at the Top like a small rounded Tower, white. The Water Course looks as if it were interrupted by the Ruins of some magnificent Castle which it had overwhelm'd. Rocks of an immense size in the Passage — near the Top $\frac{1}{2}$ a black Pillar & another not so regular above it. Island $\frac{1}{2}$ way up — the Fall close to it. The Water, obstructed by the Rocks round which it curls, falls thundering into 2 immense Gulfs just below me. On my left 2 pieces of Rock of a vast size with two Trees on each; they have been tumbled down by the Water. Never was I witness to such a Scene. As I went down, saw a hole worn thro' the Rock thro' which the Water pours black & irresistible. Skiddaw's Top shrouded

Derwentwater with Lowdore in the distance
After Thomas Allom

Honister Crag
After Joseph Farington

in Clouds & out of them down one of his seams rush'd an immense Torrent of Water quite to the Bottom of the Mountain, on which the Sun shone. The Rocks look'd wonderfully fine to-day & Lowdore at a distance particularly grand, the Water plainly alive 2 miles off, of a creamy brown, the Rocks purple, very deep, & in a recess.

Went up Borrodale thro' Rosthwaite to Sealtor[51] on the way up to the Waddmine which is on the Left when you are nearly at the Top of it. A Gush of Water the whole Way. It is very pretty looking back from the Ascent on the fertile fields of Borrodale. The Descent into Garharth[52] dale is very grand. Sublime mighty Rocks inclose the Place, that on the Right Yew Crag, that on the Left (by much the finest) Honister Crag. The Latter looks as if Waves of Rock had been violently agitated & had not yet utterly subsided. From the Top is said to be a good Prospect; when I was in the Valley the Clouds were upon it.

In Yew Crag (& some in Honister rented by the same people) vast quantities of Slate are got which is said to be of a very good Quality. The Road on the Garharth Side very bad, but not equal to the Stye. The Sledge Men come down the steepest place with Slate (at the least 40 stone in a Sledge) without prods to their Shoes, as indeed a Man told me none of them had at any time. The Noise of the Men getting Slate is said to sound like thunder. They were not at Work when I went by.

From a Gate beyond the Houses at Garharth (In the Descent you see Buttermere, the country man's Garharth Water) is a very curious View of wild Rocks & Hills: looking back the Edge of Honister Green juts out & looks like the Cone in a Crater form'd by Hay Stacks on the Right and Yew Crag on the Left, or like an Acorn in its Cup. Hay Rick & those Rocks more black & rugged than any I have seen tho' not so high as some, jagg'd & broken at the Points. The 4 Mountains that skirt the opposite Side of the Lake rise immediately from it, black, conical & immensely high & wilder than any others I have seen. Steel Pike, High Crag, Red Pike &c. Down their Sides are some wonderfully fine Waterfalls which rush at once into the Lake. Between the Hay Ricks & Steel Pikes in a Chasm in the Rock an Eagle's Nest, a remarkably fine one taken out of it this year.

This Lake about 2 miles long, very little Wood near it, & no Char in it. On the East Side close to the Water Edge some huge Hills of Rock which may perhaps have been precipitated from those on the other Side of the Road. Went to a small House, got some Honey & Bread & Butter & the afternoon being bad hasten'd home to Keswick. Took a Guide a very little way who would not take anything. Bleaberry Tarn is in the Rock or Mountain like a Crater at the North end of Garharth Water. The Mountains as one looks back at them in the Way to Keswick look dreadfully black but you soon lose sight of them & wind up the Side of the Hills that divide Buttermere from Newlands Hawse. On the Left are some Mountains like Quarter Globes green to the Top & Sheep feeding up to the Top. They look beautiful after the Barrenness of Garharth, but you see the End of one that is withdrawn from the View as black or red and grim as Grasmire. When you enter Newlands the change is wonderful. You see the Mountains on the Right as far as they be discoverable black as Night & grim as possible with many Waterfalls down them. In all the little Tarns in the very Bosoms of the Rocks are Great Quantities of Fish chiefly Trout. You go on till you come into a more cultivated country. Maiden's Bower dark & dreadful shews its back to the Right, its front is near Grange. In a low red Hill nearest you on the Right before you leave the Inclosures, Goldscop, were formerly Copper Mines but they have not been work'd for some time. About a Mile before you reach Swinside is a good view of Bassenthwaite. Got home & went to Farrington's. The Ride of the Day about 21 or 22 miles.

Thursday September 23rd

The day unpromising. Went to my Guide at Rosthwaite, who gave me an Account of the Wadd mine. He had often seen the Eagle's nest taken. He was a shepherd. The sheep will stay about the ground & Hills to which they have been us'd, & they go to fold them once or twice a week. It was very misty & uncomfortable. Went to the Left through Stonethwaite & Rosthwaite Chapel where was the

81

Schoolmaster teaching school, who has altogether an Income of £40 a year, a Rich Man.[53] When I got into the Valley the Rocks inclos'd. They look'd most tremendous, Eagle Crag (jutting forward like Castle Hill very immensely high & black as Night), Sergeant Crag & Bull Crag which (as the Guide Hutton tells you) if they be seen at all from the Part of Borrodale where strangers are generally carried it is but the Edge of each one of them which is discoverable.

When you are at this end of Borrodale, Bowfell denies all passage, & the Stake (on that Side green) is a low Hill like a Step between the posts of a Stile between far higher ones; which over, there is a passage on to Langdale. Bowfell is very high & over it from the Langdale side there is a way leading to Wastdale. The Stake is on the Left & the Road winds up it in the manner West describes. The Road is however not so bad on the Borrodale Side as many I have gone over, nor on the other so bad as the Stye for a Horse. In ascending one Place where the Earth moulders away by the side of a small Chasm & is so narrow that in leading your Horse great care is requisite to prevent his tumbling in, there is some little Danger. When you get to the top of the Stake you see one of the Tops of Langdale Pikes, Pike a Stickle, & soon come in sight of Bowfell which when I saw it partly discoverable & partly shrouded look'd black as ten Furies, terrible as Hell. On the Top is a small Valley cover'd with Ling where are great Quantities of Moor Game. People frequently come from about Kendal to shoot here. The descent into Langdale is very bad & the Road (not winding so much) is dreadfully stony, nor does it answer at all till one is at the Bottom when after proceeding a little way & looking back there is a most tremendous semicircle of Rocks: Pike a Stickle & Harrison's Pike on the Right & Bowfell in Front & a little to the Right. The foot of the Stake is about 8 miles from Ambleside or rather more. Pleasurable coming once more into a Valley that bore marks of Habitation. The Valley is a very poor one, the Soil bad & meagre. Borrodale they account better from having the Wadd mine in it. This day was a very bad one. Went by Langdale Chapel & was agreeably surpriz'd by a beautiful & true Westmoreland Lake, Elterwater, which tho' small look'd delightful from the Quantity of Charcoal

View from Langdale Pikes looking South East
After Thomas Allom

View from Langdale Pikes looking towards Bowfell
After Thomas Allom

Wood on the Hill to the Right & the Richness of the surrounding Scenery. Went by the Side of it & by Loughrigg Tarn, a diminutive Lake no way remarkable. Had a View of Windermere about 3 miles from Ambleside to which Place I went through Clapersgate.

Friday September 24th

Before Breakfast went to view the Waterfall above Ambleside. In the Morning staid at home & wrote; bad, very dark. In the afternoon went as far as the Bridge at the foot of Rydale Water, went into the inclosure & turn'd immediately to the right into a narrow lane (thro' a Gate) till I reach'd some Houses where I with some difficulty got a Boy to accompany me. (Some of the Kendal People give out Wool to be spun here.) Return'd back a few yards & turn'd to the Right up a Way which leads to Grasmere on the opposite side of the Lake to the Keswick Road. Soon came in sight of Ridale Water which from this Side looks exceedingly well with Sir Michael Fleming's[54] white House amongst the Trees & an immense Mountain tow'ring immediately above it. It look'd not like the Place of a young man of Fashion. Proceeded to where the Road joins that from Clapersgate, & turn'd to the Right. (The Ridale Road goes by the Side of Loughrigg, a great Hill, the whole way.) Went down the Lane by the Side of Grasmere water till I came to a white Gate on the Right leading to a decent House with a green field between it & the Lake nearly opposite the Island. It has a Boat House too. From this field is a beautiful View of the Lake. Went upon the Island from which the Place did not appear to Advantage & landed a little way down. Went to Grasmere & met my Horses (could have rode the whole way but 10 or 12 yards). Went up Butterlip How, but it was well nigh dark & I did not admire the View so much as I expected. A curious Waterfall in the Rock to the Left behind it. From the Side of Loughrigg you see at a great distance Saddle Back through an opening betwixt Seatandle[55] & a Mountain opposite to it. Seatandle must be part of Fairfield. It was so dark that I lost the Beauties of the Lake in my way Home.

Rydal Water near Ivy Cottage

After Thomas Allom

G R A S M E R E

From Thos. West's *Guide to the Lakes 1784*

Saturday 25th September.

The morning very bad indeed till about one o'Clock when G. Bond and I sallied out together to ascend Loughrigg. We first went to Sir Michael F.'s Park for the Cascade in the Park. It is well worth seeing & there is an excellent Road made to it. There is in it more Water than in the generality of these Falls. It consists of two falls & between them the Water curls through the Rock which forms its Channel. Went & saw the Cascade in the Orchard which is most excellently described by Mason.[56] It is best seen by stooping a little before you reach the Window when the Water appears fleecing before it passes under the Bridge. Return'd & went by the side of Ridale Water for some time the same Way as the day before. Ascended Loughrigg in the Rain & walk'd all over it in Expectation of its clearing. However we waited in Vain & walk'd at last Home wet to Skin after having been out 5 Hours or more. It clear'd up a little as we went Home & we saw Windermere from above Clapersgate but not to Advantage for we were too high.

※ ※ ※

William Wilberforce
Portrait by George Richmond

EDITOR'S EPILOGUE

'Let us hear the conclusion of the whole matter'
Ecclesiastes 12. v. 13.

Wilberforce was twenty-eight when he launched the Anti-Slave Trade Campaign. Twenty years later he won victory in the Slave Trade Abolition Act of 1807. The ensuing campaign for abolition of Slavery itself, taken over by Thomas Fowell Buxton on Wilberforce's retirement, triumphed in 1833, to be told him just three days before his death at the age of seventy three.

Pioneers of the whole movement had been 18th Century Quakers — first in U.S.A. and then in England — followed by Granville Sharp of immortal memory and James Ramsay, a martyr to the Cause. It was sustained by many others of high distinction, first among whom ranked Thomas Clarkson, indefatigable and unsparing of his health.

On page 90 is Macaulay's inscription on Wilberforce's statue in Westminster Abbey, where his body was buried next to Pitt's grave. On the opposite page is George Richmond's completed version of the portrait, that Sir Thomas Lawrence's death had left unfinished, showing Wilberforce at the age of sixty-nine, four years before he died. Richmond's picture bears a label reading:-

Statesman, Orator, Philanthropist, Saint

In his copy of George Herbert's poems Wilberforce had marked this stanza:-

Teach me, my God and King,
In all things thee to see,
And what I do in any thing,
To do it as for thee.

87

The map in Thomas West's *Guide to the Lakes, 1778.*
It is likely that Wilberforce had this with him and
then made numerous references to it in the Diary.

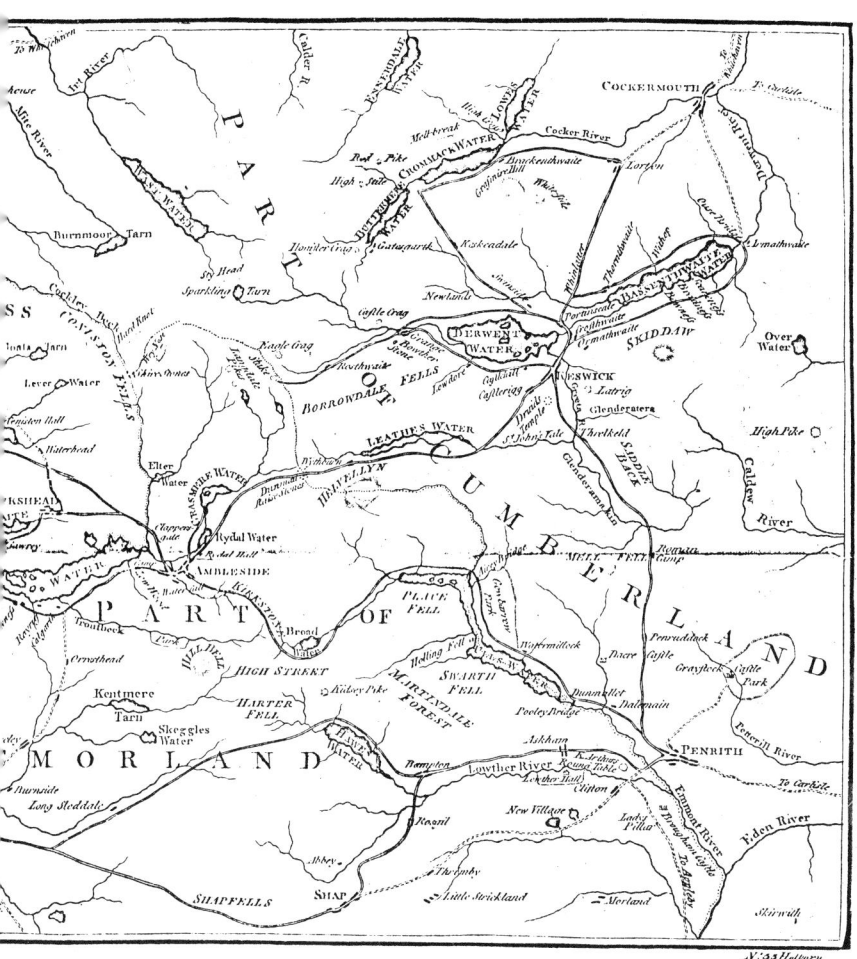

TO THE MEMORY OF

WILLIAM WILBERFORCE

(BORN IN HULL AUGUST 24TH 1759,
DIED IN LONDON JULY 29TH 1833;)
FOR NEARLY HALF A CENTURY A MEMBER OF THE HOUSE OF COMMONS,
AND, FOR SIX PARLIAMENTS DURING THAT PERIOD,
ONE OF THE TWO REPRESENTATIVES FOR YORKSHIRE.

IN AN AGE AND COUNTRY FERTILE IN GREAT AND GOOD MEN,
HE WAS AMONG THE FOREMOST OF THOSE WHO FIXED THE CHARACTER OF THEIR TIM
BECAUSE TO HIGH AND VARIOUS TALENTS
TO WARM BENEVOLENCE, AND TO UNIVERSAL CANDOUR,
HE ADDED THE ABIDING ELOQUENCE OF A CHRISTIAN LIFE.

EMINENT AS HE WAS IN EVERY DEPARTMENT OF PUBLIC LABOUR,
AND A LEADER IN EVERY WORK OF CHARITY,
WHETHER TO RELIEVE THE TEMPORAL OR THE SPIRITUAL WANTS OF HIS FELLOW MEN
HIS NAME WILL EVER BE SPECIALLY IDENTIFIED
WITH THOSE EXERTIONS
WHICH, BY THE BLESSING OF GOD, REMOVED FROM ENGLAND
THE GUILT OF THE AFRICAN SLAVE TRADE,
AND PREPARED THE WAY FOR THE ABOLITION OF SLAVERY
IN EVERY COLONY OF THE EMPIRE:

IN THE PROSECUTION OF THESE OBJECTS,
HE RELIED, NOT IN VAIN, ON GOD;
BUT IN THE PROGRESS, HE WAS CALLED TO ENDURE
GREAT OBLOQUY AND GREAT OPPOSITION:
HE OUTLIVED, HOWEVER, ALL ENMITY;
AND, IN THE EVENING OF HIS DAYS,
WITHDREW FROM PUBLIC LIFE AND PUBLIC OBSERVATION
TO THE BOSOM OF HIS FAMILY.
YET HE DIED NOT UNNOTICED OR FORGOTTEN BY HIS COUNTRY:
THE PEERS AND COMMONS OF ENGLAND,
WITH THE LORD CHANCELLOR, AND THE SPEAKER, AT THEIR HEAD,
IN SOLEMN PROCESSION FROM THEIR RESPECTIVE HOUSES,
CARRIED HIM TO HIS FITTING PLACE
AMONG THE MIGHTY DEAD AROUND,
HERE TO REPOSE:
TILL, THROUGH THE MERITS OF JESUS CHRIST,
HIS ONLY REDEEMER AND SAVIOUR,
(WHOM, IN HIS LIFE AND IN HIS WRITINGS HE HAD DESIRED TO GLORIFY,)
HE SHALL RISE IN THE RESURRECTION OF THE JUST.

Inscription on Wilberforce Memorial in Westminster Abbey

NOTES

1. Lord Sondes — he was a cousin of the Marquess, who was shortly to die childless, and he had inherited the Rockingham estates from his grandfather, the 1st Earl of Rockingham. With the marquessate went the Wentworth estates in Yorkshire, which passed to Earl Fitzwilliam.

2. Sir Jervas Clifton — the Clifton family had been there since the 12th Century, and the head of the family was commonly a 'Sir Gervase', of whom the best known, b.1587, was a gallant Cavalier who lived to see the Restoration, had seven wives and sixteen children, and inspired Shipman's poem, beginning:-

    Clifton! a name too big for verse,
    Fit only to describe his Hearse;
    Pens cannot, Trumpets should the Name reherse.

    On his second wife, a particularly charming elegy concludes:-

    Nature's Darling, Virtue's Glory,
    Thy best self is thy best story.

    The summer-house was actually built by Sir Robert Clifton in 1734.

3. Bunny Park — the Parkyns family lived there from the 16th Century, the most famous being Sir Thomas, b.1663. His passion for wrestling made Bunny the home of annual wrestling matches for a century and led him to write a most entertaining book of instruction. Then he wrote a Latin Grammar for his grandson. He became something of an expert in medicine, mathematics, architecture and hydraulics, and added much to the village buildings. His posterity, however, experienced both elevation to the Peerage and bitter matrimonial rifts, which severed the family connection early this century.

4. Colwick and Mr. Musters — the house was a mediaeval home of the Byron family, was re-built nobly in 1776 and finally became the hotel for a race-course set up in the park. Mr. Musters' son, John, was a celebrated hunting squire. He married Mary Chaworth, Byron's earliest recorded love, who died of exposure following the sack of Colwick by rioters in 1831.

5. Mr. W.'s improvements — perhaps the writer is laughing at himself.

6. Wilberfoss — the original home and name of the writer's ancestors.

7. Pocklington — the writer had lately been at school there.

8. Plumpton — he refers to the outcrop of limestone rocks, between Harrogate and Wetherby, weathered into fantastic shapes and allegedly the source of the 'Devil's Arrows' at Boroughbridge.

9. Moor Game — the writer never mentions the word 'grouse'.

10. Sunny Wit — seemingly a phonetic version of Swinithwaite.

11. Patent of Creation — i.e. when he was made Duke of Bolton. He was referring to Junius Brutus and the Tarquins.

12. Mr. Pratt — John Pratt of Askrigg was a famous and successful breeder of race-horses, had been educated at Cambridge and had inherited estates. He built a large and handsome house in the main street, part of which became the King's Arms Hotel, and his household staff were twenty in number.

13. Lib. — *libra*, i.e. lbs.

14. Meers — a measurement of leases on veins of ore. It varied from one district to another, but in Wensleydale it was 30 yards along the vein.

15. 6 pounds — the allocations must be in total, not per head.

16. Damp — i.e. fire-damp, methane.

17. A dock — the writer was a Hull man.

18. Dr. Fothergill — the Fothergill family were prosperous Quakers, who owned Carr End, near Semerwater. Dr. Fothergill had attained renown as a botanist and for his diagnosis of diphtheria. Benjamin Franklin said of him 'I can hardly conceive that a better man has ever existed'.

19. Station — the writer here means a military camp or fort, which is the sense of the place-name element '–brough'. Aggelbrough is now Addlebrough and thought to be an Iron Age fort, the cairn being the burial-place of Authulf, a British chieftain, from whom the name is derived.

20. Gastill — possibly Gearstones. His aged informant misled him about Mallerstang, which is the valley of the upper Eden, running north from the head of Wensleydale with Wild Boar Fell to its west.

21. Col. Chartres — Francis Charteris (1675 – 1732) was a notorious rogue, rake and gambler, several times mentioned by Pope on this account, and also appearing in Hogarth's *Rake's Progress*.

22. West's account — Thomas West's *Guide to the Lakes* (London 1778). The writer mentions it often, particularly its recommended 'stations' or viewpoints. West was a Scot who became a Jesuit and in that profession was sent to work in the north-west of England.

23. Wrynose and Hardknot — hills perhaps hardly so conspicuous as to be mentioned, unless the writer already knew them from a previous visit.

24. Mr. P. — a Mr. Pocklington, who had recently built a house on one of the islands in Derwentwater.

25. Gray — Thomas Gray, the poet, had visited the Lakes in 1769 and was something of a pioneer in his appreciation of the countryside, as his Journal shows. (See note 56 on W. Mason.)

    His account of Lowdore fall runs:-

    ' — *the stream was nobly broken, leaping from rock to rock, and foaming with fury. On one side a towering crag that spired up to equal, if not overtop the neighboring cliffs (this lay all in shade and darkness): on the other hand a rounder broader projecting hill shagged with wood, and illuminated by the sun, which glanced sideways on the upper part of the cataract.*'

26. Salvator — Salvator Rosa (1615-73); his landscape paintings were much admired in England at the time, and the comparison with the scenery around Keswick had already been made by other writers, e.g. West.

27. Glass — the Claude glass or Claude Lorraine glass was a slightly convex and darkened or coloured hand-mirror. Admirers of the 'picturesque' liked to view their scenery in one of these in order to give the landscape the proportions of a picture in a frame.

28. Great Gavel — Great Gable; both versions were in use a century later, see Black's *Guide to the Lakes*, 16th edition, 1870, pp. 221 and 224.

29. Wadd Mine — once a famous source of graphite, no longer worked.

30. Caleb Fisher — the writer left a space here for the name which was never filled in. It has been supplied from a note in Joseph Farington's second collection of Lakeland Views (1816) where the author of the text, T. H. Horne, says that Mr. Fisher in old age was still entertaining tourists with his account of the poet's visit.

31. Foe Park — Fawe Park.

32. Lady's Bower — seemingly one of several names for Maiden's Moor.

33. Goose Gate, Whittle Gate etc. — West mentions 'clog-shoes, harden-sark, whittle-gate and goose-gate', sceptically, as perquisites of the incumbent of the parish.

34. Dr. Brownrigg — Dr. William Brownrigg (1711–1800) had retired to his family house at Ormathwaite after a fascinating practise at Whitehaven, where he had made himself the leading authority on mine gases. He also was a friend of Benjamin Franklin, with whom he experimented in stilling Derwent-water during a storm by pouring oil on the water.

35. Farrington — almost certainly this is Joseph Farington (1747–1821) the landscape painter, who was living in Keswick from 1776 to 1781. He published two collections of engravings of the scenery of the Lakes. (p.45 *sqq*)

36. Briareus — he had 100 hands and 50 heads, as befitted a son of Heaven and Earth. His exploits with and against the gods were numerous, and he may be custodian of the Titans in Tartarus, but it seems more likely that he is still buried under Mt. Etna.

37. Ewsbridge — phonetic spelling of Ousebridge.

38. Wildthorpe — now Wythop.

39. Scruffel — the mountain Criffell, in Kirkcudbrightshire.

40. Brydone's account — Patrick Brydone (1741–1818) was a traveller and writer from Berwickshire.

41. The Crescent — he is clearly describing some prismatic effect of a telescope.

42. Horseing Stone at the Vicarage — this was one of Gray's and West's 'stations'.

43. like that at Middleham — i.e. yet another echo.

44. A force seemingly inadequate — all the cannon had been spiked the year before by the renegade, Paul Jones, formerly an apprentice at Whitehaven, when in an American privateer he attempted a raid which was foiled by one of his own gang warning the inhabitants. Like Napoleon's at Les Invalides, but less deservedly, his body is entombed in marble, at the Naval Chapel of Annapolis, Maryland, U.S.A.

45. Mr. Lutwidge — Charles Lutwidge Esq. of Whitehaven was surveyor & controller-general of the coast of Cumberland & Westmorland. His property included the estate of Holmrook near Ravenglass, which later passed to his nephew Major Charles Lutwidge who was controller of customs at Hull. Major Lutwidge's daughter Frances Jane was the mother of Lewis Carroll. His eldest son, another Charles — this time the Rev. Charles Lutwidge — was eventually to exchange livings with the Rev. Robert Wilberforce, the writer's second son (the living of Burton Agnes in Yorkshire for that of East Farleigh in Kent).

46. Sir James Lowther's Place — presumably Whitehaven Castle.

47. Shivers — fractured pieces of stone.

48. End — Great End.

49. Shalloons — the O.E.D. gives 'a closely woven material chiefly used for linings'. Conceivably they were blankets, which elsewhere were called 'chalons'.

50. Burgage Tenures — it was the votes attached to such yearly rentals that enabled Sir James Lowther to get William Pitt elected MP for Appleby in the following year.

51. Sealtor — perhaps Seatoller.

52. Garharth — Gatescarth or Gatesgarth, as now written.

53. A rich man —
    A man he was to all the country dear,
    And passing rich with forty pounds a year.
    Goldsmith, *The Deserted Village*, 1770

54. Sir Michael Fleming — 4th baronet of a family living at Rydal Hall since 1600 or earlier: labelled 'the brilliant baronet' by Sir Walter Scott for his social and literary gifts, the former of which Wilberforce found rather excessive in later days, when he himself stayed in his rented house, Rayrigg, on Windermere, which was also a Fleming property.

55. Seatandle — i.e. Seat Sandal, the mountain opposite being Dollywaggon Pike.

56. Mason — William Mason (1724–97), rector of Aston near Rotherham, was a friend of Thomas Gray and after his death published *The Poems of Mr. Gray to which are prefixed Memoirs of his Life and Writings* (York 1775). The memoirs included the journal of Gray's visit to the Lakes, actually written as a series of letters to another friend who had hoped to accompany him. The writer is here referring to one of Mason's notes to Gray's journal:-

    '— *A small waterfall visible only through the window of a ruined summer-house in Sir Michael's orchard. Here Nature has performed every thing in little that she usually executes on her largest scale; and on that account, like the miniature painter, seems to have finished every part of it in a studied manner; not a little fragment of rock thrown into the bason, not a single stem of brushwood that starts from its craggy sides but has its picturesque meaning; and the little central stream dashing down a cleft of the darkest-coloured stone, produces an effect of light and shadow beautiful beyond description. This little theatrical scene might be painted as large as the original, on a canvas not bigger than those which are usually dropped in the Opera-house.*'